INTO THE UNKNOWN

*A Journey of Courage,
Risk, and Faith*

BY

YVONNE ELLIS

Bible scripture Quotations are taken from the New King James Version of the Bible.

www.yemeempowerment.com

Yvonne Ellis/Into The Unknown

ISBN: 978-1-9998590-2-2

ACKNOWLEDGEMENTS

I give all the honour, praise, and glory to The Living God through His son Jesus Christ for transforming my life and making me the woman I am today.

My darling husband, Stephen, thank you for supporting me even when it's been challenging. One day all our hard work will pay off. And all that we planned, dreamed, and talked about over the last 16 years on our romantic walks will become a reality.

I will always love you, Tennika.

My Darling Jada, thank you for always being an encouragement and blessing to me. I hope through seeing my life in action, you will know it is possible to live your dream. Love always, Mama.

Sister Pauline. Thank you for all you have done for me.

Ije, you encouraged me to dream big with God and rely on Him no matter the challenges. Thank you for your friendship, prayers, and advice.

Thank you, Marcia, for all your support. I hope my journey encourages you to take a leap of faith.

Thank you, C.B, Caroline, Doretta, Andrena, Judith, and the ladies at Christ Church Orpington for encouraging, supporting, and praying for me. God bless you all.

Fabi, God bless you.

Sheree, thank you for your mentorship, guidance, and encouragement over the years.

Victor and Adriana, God bless you always for the kindness and support you gave me during my stay in California.

CONTENTS

FOREWORD

Life is all about trying new things and seizing opportunities. It could be learning a new skill, visiting a new country, putting yourself forward for something you have never done before, or doing something totally outside your comfort zone. It can feel scary. You may wonder if you can do it. You may think about what people might say about you. Thoughts of failure may cross your mind. I have experienced all these thoughts and feelings while doing new things.

Through my different experiences of stepping out into the unknown, I have discovered that to get to the next level, break free of whatever is holding you back in life, or achieve the extraordinary and do something amazing in life, it takes courage and risk to achieve it.

When I talk about risk, I am not talking about reckless risk, which involves being impulsive or to the detriment of others. I am talking about risk that involves knowing there is a cost, give or take, calculating it, and moving forward, not knowing the exact outcome. *For which of you, intending to build a tower does not sit down first and count the cost, whether he has enough* to finish *it?* **(Luke 14:28)**

I remember taking my first risk at 13 years old. I told someone that my dad was sexually abusing me. I did not know where my decision to speak out would take me. I knew there would be a consequence. Even with the threats (my dad telling me at ten years old that if I ever told anyone what he was doing to me, I would go deaf, dumb, and blind), I still decided to take a risk. I had limited understanding at such a young age of what my decision to tell would mean for my life, but I knew that my life would change: I just didn't know how. That was the first time I took a step into the unknown. And I have been living a life of courage and risk ever since.

My journey of faith started with God at twenty-one years old when I began a personal relationship with Jesus Christ. Being a follower of Christ has given me first-hand experience of the journey of courage, risk, and faith combined in action. Talk about hands-on experience! If I am honest, stepping out into the unknown has been extremely hard. But as I have taken each step with faith, I have learned to be risk-tolerant rather than risk-averse.

To fulfil my purpose and vision, to become a woman of greatness that I was called to be, I must fully explore my potential by continuing to break out of my comfort zone. I must continue to resist the temptation to live within people's expectations. To break out of the constraints that society would have me believe about myself due to my background. I cannot do it in my strength. I ask God for the courage, confidence, and guidance to do all he believes I can do.

I hope as you read my book you will be inspired by my journey and that it encourages you to take a risk to step out into your unknown. Hopefully, despite whatever fears, insecurities, or doubts that may linger in your mind, you will see from my story it is not in the absence of these feelings you will achieve new things, but in spite of them. It is possible to break into new territory and achieve your dreams.

Yvonne

"With men this is impossible,
but *with God all things are possible"*
(Matthew 19:26).

CHAPTER ONE
TRUST WITHOUT BORDERS

There is a song that I used to sing during my prayer and worship time with God. A particular line would always stand out to me. It touched my soul. It goes: "Spirit lead me where my trust is without borders. Let me walk upon the waters, wherever you would call me".

So profound are the words and powerful. I would sing them with passion aloud in the early dawn of the morning, longing in my heart to desperately escape the mundane routine that my life had become.

I longed for a different direction in my life. I wanted an adventure. Up until this point, in March 2017, I had already achieved many great things. I was an author, founder, and director of a peer empowerment organisation called Daughter Arise, a wife and mother. However, it was during my enrolment on a leadership program that I realised there was something more I was meant to be doing with my life.

At the time, I worked part-time for Wandsworth Council as an administrator in children's services. Even how I ended up in that job was a surreal experience. And it was off the back of another period in my life where I had again stepped out into the unknown. I had left my last job ten months before. I worked as an Interview Officer for the Home Office for five years (I will tell you more about that later). My ten-month hiatus from employment had, at times, been an angst-ridden but clarity-inducing period of my life, even though I was not exactly sure where my life or career was going.

One morning I decided to visit a temp agency for the first time. For those of you that are not familiar with what a temp agency is, it is a job agency that finds you temporary or contract work in a short amount of time. I was at a point financially where I needed a job. As I sat waiting patiently to see the job consultant, I filled in the forms and re-checked that I had my CV and correct identity documents.

The Consultant asked me what type of job I was looking for. I responded that I was looking for something part-time.

"I have the perfect job for you," she said. "Funnily enough, jobs like this never come into the agency, and it came in this morning."

Wandsworth Children Services had a job post for an administrator. It was only 18 hours a week; I wanted thirty hours. But as I needed to have some type of income again and a job that would fit in with my other commitments, I agreed to go for an interview.

Two days later, I went for the interview. Two of us, both women, were shortlisted to interview for the post. The Interviewer, who was also the Manager of the department, said we both did so well in our interview that she decided to make two posts available. I ended up working as an administrator for the Fostering Team. The slow realisation of the department I was working in left me shocked. Imagine ending up working for the same department you were fostered in as a child! Twenty-five years before, I was a child of the state, in care and looked after by this local government authority. I was emotional the first few weeks on the job. How did I end up walking into a job agency that found me a job back at the place where my journey into the unknown first began? I could not figure it out, but I believed God mysteriously had a hand in it. There was a reason why He put me here.

I made sure that I did my job to the best of my ability and that even the little tasks were done properly. One of my responsibilities was to ensure the medical files for Looked After Children's medical were correctly maintained. That brought back memories. I remember when I received my files from my time in care ten years after I left. They arrived in the post with the envelope tattered and falling apart. The files were also not correctly labelled with my name, and the pages were falling out. On seeing the state of some of the children's files, I was reminded of this. And how that memory brought back the feeling of how insignificant I felt during my time in the care system. It's funny how

I connected that feeling to the way my file arrived on my doorstep. I doubted that was the intention of the person that sent it. It may seem an irrelevant thing to think about to other people, but I did not want any young person whose medical files I was responsible for maintaining to receive their file like that. I wanted them to see it was treated with care. I took my job seriously because I remembered what it was like to be a child in care. I considered it a great honour to work for the fostering team. Every time I walked into the office; I was pleasantly reminded of how far I had come.

I learned a lot about specialist administration, and for the first two years, I was constantly challenged. It was enjoyable and interesting because I was learning new skills and getting invaluable experience that would further help me in my life and pursuits. I did such a good job that the Business Manager increased my hours from eighteen to twenty-four and eventually to thirty hours which is what I originally wanted. My job ticked all the right and convenient boxes, but as the years went by, I grew restless.

I was always blessed to have great part-time jobs that fit around my children's schooling. I believed from a young age that someone from my disadvantaged background (coming from a broken family and the care system) would do well to grab any opportunity that came my way. I worked my way up from the bottom. I left care at seventeen years old as a single mom with one GCSE A+ qualification in English to my name. Everything that I have achieved has come through hard work, determination, and the favour of God. I refused to lose even though there were times when I temporarily gave in.

I naively thought for many years that if I worked hard enough, someone in whatever company I worked for would recognise my potential and that in turn would create better opportunities for me. I was a diligent and hard worker who always worked with excellence. In part, my potential was recognised, but it was never enough to earn me a promotion or, at times, even a chance to do something different to my job role. I was disappointed for a long time with my career, but I learned as the years went by that in the modern job world, and life in general that to get ahead, it is not what you know but whom you know. My face never did fit in, and I never wanted to be part of a clique, so that pre-requisite automatically disqualified me before I even got a foot on the ladder. I grew discouraged and disillusioned with the traditional career path, but I still stuck with it because that was what I was used to, and well, I needed a paycheque. I was nearly forty years old when it finally dawned on me that traditional employment (working for a direct employer) was not right for me. I knew I could achieve more. But what would I do next?

I didn't exactly know what, but I wanted to do something big and bold, something that would not only transform my life but the lives of others too. I started to think about setting up a company that would facilitate the empowerment of people through a range of services and resources. I believed that I could make a difference; I saw that through my charitable work with Daughter Arise. I discovered from the emails and many wonderful conversations I had with different people that I inspired and empowered them through my life story. I realised I had the gift of empowerment and knew that my purpose and calling were tied to it. The problem was that even though I had the right desire to want life change, I lacked courage, confidence, and self-belief. I knew these were key to me achieving the dreams I had in my heart, and

I knew only God could help me gain the confidence that I needed. Little did I realise that the words of the song that I sometimes sang during my prayer time with God were about to be put to the test in my life. I was about to find out what it truly means to trust in God.

One evening in January 2017, as I was spending quiet time with God, I told him that I wanted to do a TED talk. So, imagine my surprise the next day when I opened my hot mail account to find an email from TEDx Wandsworth. TEDx is part of TED talks, a world-renowned platform that allows speakers to present on a topic that they are both passionate and knowledgeable about. I was so excited to see the email. I knew this could be a huge opportunity for me, so I decided to go for it. I remember back in 2013, when I started work as an administrator for children's services, an ex-colleague that had read my book, *Daughter Arise*, suggested I should do a TED talk. At the time, I was petrified at the prospect of doing a talk on such a respected platform, even though at the time, I was a quite confident as a public speaker with four years' experience under my belt. I was used to sharing my story with a range of different audiences, but

I felt intimidated by the prestige of TED talks. I felt I would not measure up to their standard and that no one would be interested in what I had to say (There goes that lack of self-belief again rearing its ugly head).

At the time, I put that initial conversation with my colleague to the back of my mind, and I continued to do public speaking as and when people requested it. But over time, as my confidence and self-belief started to grow with every new accomplishment that I achieved, my view of myself changed. This was a pivotal part of my transformation. I wasn't scared anymore, nor did I view myself as less than others that applied for this opportunity. I believed I had something of value to offer. As I excitedly opened the email attachment to fill in the application form, I knew I had nothing to lose but everything to gain. I had in my favour that I knew my topic very well. Not only had I lived through the topic I was going to present solutions about, but I also publicly spoke about the topic, and I was the founder of an organisation that successfully helped people with my solutions. My biggest challenge was having courage because I had never attempted anything of this magnitude before.

The process of being selected as a TEDx speaker was the beginning of my development. From submitting my application to doing the audition, I battled with my introverted nature. I had three minutes to deliver my pitch for the idea of my talk. I had to be precise and concise. Planning my pitch and doing the audition helped me sharpened my thought process and talking technique as a speaker. Obviously, as an inspirational speaker, I had spoken in front of audiences before but to be in a room with other speakers vying for one of the prized sixteen places made the experience extremely nerve-racking. My husband, Stephen, and my daughter Jada accompanied me to give moral support. I felt greatly encouraged.

Nerves had me shaking on the inside, but as I stood on the stage, I harnessed the feeling and turned it into power. I was focused, and I was not going to let anything get in the way of me being selected as a TEDx speaker. This was a special opportunity, and I was not going to blow it. I delivered my talk in the 3 minutes allocated and covered all the points. A couple of weeks later, I was informed by email that I was selected as one of the sixteen speakers. I was so happy. I could not believe something like this could happen to me. Dreams do come true.

My TEDx talk was about how people can empower survivors of childhood sexual abuse and highlighting the challenges survivors face. Over the next six months, I worked tirelessly on my presentation and delivery. I spent time gathering research and used my findings from research papers and my work in this field to back up my theory. The process was rigorous and challenging, but I enjoyed it as I developed my knowledge and the constant practice helped me become a better speaker. It was invaluable to have the access, insight, and expertise of the TEDx Wandsworth team.

2017 continued to be a year of stepping into the unknown. Besides preparing for the TEDx talk in November that year, I was also preparing to share my personal sexual abuse story on the streets of Brixton, London. It all started a year before when I saw a street preacher outside Clapham Common tube station. He was sharing the gospel of Jesus Christ through a megaphone. An unfamiliar thought came to me that I should buy a megaphone and do something similar and share my story in public. Immediately I thought what a bizarre thought to have, but then I started thinking about where I could buy a megaphone. Six months later, the thought crossed my mind again, and I realised God was prompting me to take a step of courage to do it. So, in April 2017, I raised the £235.00 needed to buy the equipment, refreshments, and t-shirts for my team of six volunteers and me. I raised the money in one month, and by the end of May, we were ready to hit the streets of Brixton. Again, I was nervous about doing something so unfamiliar to me. I didn't think I would have the courage to go through with it. I prepared for the event by fasting and praying, and I believed in faith that many people would be touched by what I was going to share. June 7th, 2017 was the day I did the Testimony to the street event. Nerves tried to get the better of me, but the volunteers prayed for me. As I lifted the megaphone to my mouth outside Ritzy cinema in Brixton, a calm boldness overtook me. It was no easy feat speaking through a megaphone as people crossed the road with the pedestrian lights changing every few minutes. I had to keep going back to the beginning of my story as new people passed by. It was an amazing experience, and the volunteers had interesting conversations with a range of different people. They also gave out over 300 leaflets as I shared my story. I had a few hecklers where I was standing only because it was the local hang-out spot for drunks and drug addicts, but I did not let that faze me. By the end of the two hours of speaking through that megaphone, my throat was sore, but I achieved my aim: to tell people there is hope after childhood sexual abuse.

My confidence skyrocketed after doing the street event. I started to realise a pattern was emerging in my life, and that was in new, challenging situations that required me to take a risk; I had to be courageous and bold. Honestly, it was a strange experience. I was living a life of two different halves. In my day-to-day life, I lived in a comfort zone of having a secure job, knowing what each day would more or less bring, but outside of work, I was living a courageous life seizing opportunities and taking risks.

As the months passed, I continued to juggle both worlds. I prepared for my TEDx talk in between working, looking after my family, running my charitable organisation, and preparing for my leadership exam. Yes, you read right: In the background of all I have shared with you thus far, I was in the process of completing a leadership program in ministry and public life with Phoebe Academy through the Institute of Leadership and Management. It was while doing this program I started to sense that I was called to be a global leader. It sounds unbelievable, doesn't it? That I, Yvonne Ellis, the girl that came from a broken background of terrible childhood sexual abuse, who for many years lived a life of dysfunction could ever be in such a position?

What can I say? Nothing is impossible with God. I started to see myself not as I was but as someone with great potential. No doubt had I said such statements aloud, most people would have laughed at me, even think I was deluded for thinking so highly of myself. But at Phoebe academy, it was normal to view yourself that way because we were taught to view ourselves from God's viewpoint. I read my bible, and I believe what God said about me. Because despite how I look on the outside and regardless of my broken beginning, I know I have been called by God to do amazing outlandish things. All that has unfolded in my life thus far is for a very specific purpose.

The night before the TEDx talk, I practised as I prepared my outfit. I decided to wear something smart but comfortable. I opted for a royal blue jumper and cigarette trousers (called that name because of the slim leg fit). I was focused on delivering a great talk the next day; I felt quietly confident. Up to this point, I had been practising for six weeks straight, morning and night. Every moment was an opportunity to practice as I sat at the bus stop waiting for a bus to go to work, as I cooked dinner, and in my bed getting ready to go to sleep. I even roped in my daughter Jada to help me prepare by getting her to time me on a stopwatch to ensure I kept within the set timeframe. I attended the pre-rehearsal the day before. I had prepared my best; now, it was up to God to do the rest. All that was left for me to do now was turn up and talk.

I slept only a few hours and was up at 6 am. I was not due to be at the venue until 11 am, but I could not sleep any longer. As I had my cup of tea in the kitchen leaning against the counter, I practised my talk for what seemed like the hundredth time using the cooker timer as my stopwatch. Before I knew it, it was time to drop off

Jada at her aunt's house. My husband and I then
made our way to the venue.

I had been to South Thames College once
before when my employers held the annual staff
conference there. The bus that took me to my job
as an administrator dropped me at the stop outside
the college. This was where the TEDx event was
taking place. I didn't realise it had a theatre inside.
As I booked in, I was surprised by the number
of people in attendance. There were people from
different backgrounds that came from different
areas around the country to attend, not just people
in Wandsworth.

My husband and I took our seats in the theatre
along with the other 100 people that attended the
TEDx event. I was third in line to present my talk.
Before I knew it, I was called to the stage. Amman,
the TEDx organiser, gave me such a warm welcome
it helped put me at ease. The time had now come. I
took a deep breath. Under the dimmed lights of the
darkened theatre, I could see all eyes were on me.
The audience was dead silent as they waited with
bated breath for me to say the first words of my talk.
It's hard to describe the atmosphere of anticipation
that hung in the air; it was almost palpable. I was

nervous, and I must admit slightly scared, but as always, I converted my nervousness and fear into power. I glanced at the clock. The countdown timer was set for eighteen minutes. I took a deep breath and began my presentation. I imagined this feeling must be like jumping out of a plane waiting for the parachute to open. The pressure and exhilaration ran through me simultaneously as I tried to keep focused. As I talked, I remembered my stage presence, maintaining eye contact with the audience as I walked to and fro. Then stage fright happened. I suddenly froze for a few seconds, but it felt like a lifetime. The audience remained silent as I gathered myself. This talk was extremely personal for me. Not only had I lived through the trauma of sexual abuse, but I was also trying to articulate for those who had not found their voice why they struggled with their secret. At that moment, I felt vulnerable, almost childlike. It was only for a moment, but as I remembered why I was here doing this talk, I finished well and strong. With each point I made, power arose within me. The passion I felt for the cause carried me through. I completed my talk.

The audience rose to their feet, and I received a standing ovation. I was so emotional and thankful for this beautiful opportunity. Afterwards, in the meet and greet area, many attendees came up to me and congratulated me on my talk. It was amazing to hear how it was received and what people took away from it. My husband was so proud of me, and I was glad to share this experience with him. I was walking on air for months afterwards. It further affirmed to me that to experience extraordinary opportunities such as this, you must take a risk and have courage. It also confirmed to me that the life God wants me to live is outside my comfort zone. How could I continue to settle for living a life of comfort?

CHAPTER TWO
TIME TO TAKE ACTION

After several tastes of courageous living, my comfort life was starting to bother me. The contrast was evident: I went from doing a life-changing TEDx talk and graduating from a leadership program to standing at a photocopier at eight in the morning scanning medical forms. Something about my life was not adding up.

As I prepared the pages of each form for scanning (usually, there would be at least twenty 12-page forms), I daydreamed about what had been an amazing few weeks. My family and friends came to celebrate my graduation with me at Phoebe academy. It was a wonderful day. Pastor Eric, the President of the academy, asked me to give a speech to the other graduates and guests in attendance.

On presenting me with my certificate, he said, "Here stands a global leader. Soon, you will need an appointment to see Yvonne." I was greatly honoured to receive such a prophecy and acclamation. I was going to miss attending the academy.

For seven months of my life, it was a great source of inspiration and encouragement for me. I enjoyed attending the classes, and I was always enthusiastic about learning. I only missed one class (that was because of the street event I did in Brixton). I gained so much from being in the program. I learned about servant leadership and what it meant to be a Godly Leader.

2017 proved to be the best and most adventurous year of my life. It was a year of personal transition. My outlook on life would never be the same again. I had tasted what was possible if I stepped out of my comfort zone to try new things. I decided as I stood at the photocopier that it was time to act. No longer was I willing to settle for less.

I kept saying I would leave my job, yet here I still was. I promised myself at the beginning of this employment I would not be here longer than five years (at this point, I was now three and a half years in). It wasn't for the lack of trying. Towards the end of 2016, I applied for a couple of caseworker jobs working with women, but I didn't get an interview. I also applied simultaneously for two administrator jobs with the Church of England. They had set up a new department to respond to the findings of the Independent Inquiry into child sexual abuse. I thought it would be a good experience for me because of the voluntary work I was doing to support survivors of childhood sexual abuse and because I am a Christian. I thought that whilst I figured out my next move, if I could get a job in line with my passion and interests, maybe I wouldn't get bored so easily. However, my attempts were half-hearted because I didn't want to step into another job that would lead nowhere career-wise for me.

People that know me well will tell you that I am not the type of person to sit by idly twiddling my thumbs, waiting for things to happen. This is my nature. I am a woman that loves to work and do creative, meaningful things. Even when none of my best-laid plans worked out, I spent every spare minute I had in between my paid job, family, and other commitments pursuing activities that built my self-development, knowledge, and skills. At work on my lunch break, I would listen to podcasts by different entrepreneurs on my iPhone rather than get involved in office gossip. My usual mundane bus ride to and from work became a space where I wrote ideas in my snazzy notebook (I love good stationery!) and planned my new business goals. The company logo for my business YEME Empowerment was created on the 37 bus!

I spent all my time daydreaming at work about my plans and dreams. It provided me with motivation and positive escapism from my job, as the workplace was such a toxic environment. My accomplishments turned me into a dreamer. I started to dream of achieving great things. As I grew in confidence, self-belief, and knowledge, I believed it was possible as I read stories of other people that rose from disadvantaged and small beginnings. I spent most of my time reading books by people such as John Maxwell, Myles Munroe, Dr. Dennis Kimbro, Dale Carnegie, and others. And I was greatly inspired by entrepreneurs such as Sophie Amoruso, Maria Hatisfazis, and Carrie H. Johnson, as their stories showed me with determination and hard work, it is possible to live your dream.

To people looking in from the outside, what I've achieved in my life may seem like no big deal, but to me, it is massive. Twenty-two years ago, when I was in a mental health facility staring out of metal barred windows, I thought my life was over. I had given up hope that things would ever get better for me. I am greatly motivated by my achievements because I never thought I would do all the things I have done thus far. It always fills me with complete joy when I accomplish something new or overcome a particularly hard challenge. Who would believe that I would achieve all that I have done given my background? At one point, I certainly did not think so and not the people that had written me off as a lost cause a long time ago. Thankfully God didn't write me off. He gave me the confidence to believe that I could do more than I could ask or imagine because His power lives within me. *"Now to him who is able to do immeasurably more than all we ask or imagine, according to his power that is at work within us"* **(Ephesians 3:20).**

It was because of this confidence and the realisation that I had come to the end of the road in my day job that started me on the process of attempting to leave my job again. It was scary making such a tough decision, but it was the right thing to do. I spent many evenings in the lead-up to having a discussion with my husband praying and seeking God for confirmation. And God did confirm in many ways that I was on the right path. For example, one evening, I was at my friend's house. We were discussing the pros and cons of me leaving the security of a paid job. My friend, like me, is a deeply spiritual (not religious) woman (meaning before she acts, she will pray and seek God's wisdom first). As we were talking, I felt led to pray about the situation, so we prayed together. A bible scripture came to mind: *"Whether you turn to the right or to the left, your ears will hear a voice behind you, saying, This is the way; walk in it"* (**Isaiah 30:21**). I took this as a sign I was going in the right direction.

The second confirmation came via a book by author Jackie Pullinger called Chasing the Dragon. I had read her book a couple of years before, and I was greatly inspired by her courage and faith to step out into the unknown to do what people would consider "impossible."

Jackie was a young student in her twenties when she answered the call of God to go to Hong Kong to be a missionary. She tried all the traditional avenues of applying to embassies abroad, but she was turned down. A church minister who sought counsel from time to time encouraged her to go forward and trust God to lead her. So, she boarded a boat to Hong Kong with her oboe (musical instrument) and little money to her name. She stepped out in faith against all odds and trusted God to provide for her: and He did.

On reading her story a second time, I came across two things that I had not noticed before. Firstly, courage and risk are needed if you want to do great and remarkable things. Secondly, faith, trust, and guidance from God will help you to do it. "*Trust in the Lord* with all your heart *and lean not on your own understanding; in all your ways submit to him, and he will make your paths straight*" **(Proverbs 3:5-6).**

But trusting God in practice was not what I was doing. Instead, I worried and tried to figure out how I was going to get enough income once I left my job and what I was going to do to get work. I spent late evenings searching on the internet for testimonies of other Christians that had taken similar paths. At the time, I suppose I was looking for some type of reassurance that everything would turn out okay even though I anticipated there would be challenges.

I finally dared to tell my husband that I believed God had shown me it was time to leave my job. I asked him what he thought. His opinion mattered a lot to me; after all, we were married and had been through so much together. The last thing I wanted to do was bring harm or hardship to my family, but I sensed if I stepped out to start my own business and follow the path that God had planned for me, it would initially be the case. I cried as I shared my fears with my husband as he stood at my office door. His response gave me some reassurance as he told me he had never seen anyone that wanted to please God like me, and because of that, he knew I would not have taken such a decision lightly. I was quietly relieved that he backed my decision even though I did not know fully what I would do for income after I left my job.

The day after the conversation with my husband, I typed up my resignation letter. I had it all prepared to give it to my manager. I only had to give one month's notice: the time would fly by quickly. I had been waiting for this day to leave for the best part of a year, and I felt a huge relief that the time had come. I started to clear files on my computer at work and got rid of the large number of emails that accumulated in my inbox over the years. I was planning on leaving quietly. But a few days before I was due to hand in my notice, I faced a huge setback; my husband changed his mind and no longer supported my decision to leave. I was devastated at his change of heart; I was relying on his support, but I could understand his concerns. My husband said that I should not leave unless I had something in place and suggested that I sign up to a temporary job agency as I did before. It seemed to make sense, and I did not want to disrespect my husband, so I decided to honour his request. I rang a few job agencies to see if I could get on their books ahead of me leaving my job as my husband told me a couple of his colleagues had done this. However, all the agencies I spoke to said I would have to leave first. I became increasingly unhappy and restless.

I felt stuck in between a rock and a hard place. Stuck between doing what I believed God wanted me to do and staying in a job well past its expiration date because of financial commitments. I did not want to put additional stress on my family. I continued to pray to God for confirmation even though I already knew the direction I was supposed to take. One of the signs I always felt when I was on the right track with God is inner peace. But in staying put, I could not settle, and the more I tried to use my understanding to work out a way to leave smoothly and comfortably, the more confusing and frustrating the situation became.

One evening as I was working on my projects at home, I decided that I would contact the Chief Executive of Richmond and Wandsworth Council and Heads of Service at my workplace to tell them about my achievements. I made a flow chart of all the people that I would contact and put space under their names for the outcome of each meeting. Ideally, I was thinking, as I was once a Looked After Child under this local authority, maybe they would be interested in my story and that it could possibly lead to an opportunity to do something different. After all, as the saying goes, if you don't ask, you don't get, right? Nothing was ever handed to me on a platter, and I was used to creating my opportunities. Therefore, it was nothing for me to do this.

In August 2017, I wrote the email to the Chief Executive. I told him about my journey of how I came into government care under Wandsworth Children Services. I also told him about my TEDx talk. In the email, I put links to my peer empowerment organisation, Daughter Arise, the TEDx talk, and my book. I copied the email to the director of Children Services and the assistant director. Once I spell-checked my email, I hit the send button.

Six weeks had passed since I sent the email, and I received no response. I checked the junk folders of both my work and personal email to see if anything had landed in there but to no avail. I was not disappointed because I had done what I said I was going to do. At least I tried. I reasoned that the Chief Executive was probably too busy to get back to me anyway.

Imagine my surprise eight weeks after I sent the email, I logged into my work computer to find that he replied! His email was very courteous, and he invited me to meet with him. Even though I had no expectations when sending the email to get this, it was very encouraging. I wasted no time in responding to the invite, and as requested, I contacted his Personal Assistant to arrange the appointment.

On the day of the meeting, I was a bit nervous but prepared. I brought a copy of my autobiography, Daughter Arise, to show him. His Assistant assured me he was very down to earth as she offered me a glass of water. I was sitting outside his office for a short time before he called me in.

Paul (that was his name) was, as his assistant said, very down to earth. He was not what I expected from someone in such a high position. I expected him to be quite aloof and formal, but instead, he was friendly, professional, and not with all the formalities. Our conversation covered various topics. I told him about how I came to be in care and my journey through the care system, and how I got to be where I was today. I shared with him my bizarre story of how I ended up working for the fostering team (the same department I was in care under three decades before). He was quite surprised that my experiences and skills had not been utilised whilst working in my admin job. I told him people had always known about my achievements, but I explained that once people fit you in a mould, your chances are limited.

I explained that as I was employed as an "administrator," no one was willing to give me a chance to do anything else. It did seem to me that there was an unseen class system. In the first three years of my employment, when I tried to take an interest in doing certain courses to learn different things, I was told I could not as I was an 'administrator.' The career path was narrow, and unless I wanted to train to become a social worker, there were no other options to expand. The chief executive seemed to understand my dilemma.

We talked about my work with survivors of childhood sexual abuse and news stories in the press surrounding it. I was able to share my knowledge on a topic that he had a basic understanding of, and he keenly listened to my opinions and ideas of possible solutions to the problem. The hour passed quickly. As I was getting ready to leave, he asked if he could read my book and promised to return it. I gave it to him and left the meeting.

As I walked back to work, I reflected on what was a positive meeting. It made me realise that no matter the title or position that a person holds, we can all learn something from each other. The meeting reaffirmed to me that I have something of great value to bring to all people, my knowledge, and it's not only for survivors of abuse. For a long time, I had doubted the value of my experiences and my knowledge based on other people's views of me. On numerous occasions, directly and indirectly, various people told me because I did not have a title, position, or qualifications, my speaking on certain subjects was invalid.

My entire life, I have always been defined by a label. When I was in care, I was a 'care kid.' After I was sexually abused, I became the 'survivor.' And the negative connotation that came along with that title and experience meant I was supposed to be broken beyond repair emotionally and psychologically, and never expected to be the exception, only the norm; only to survive my experience, not thrive. And let me not forget the label given to me by various jobs roles that excluded me from being able to pursue other opportunities. At different points in my life, these labels affected my confidence and self-belief, but I always had a sense that my identity was never based on them. My identity comes from God alone.

A week after my meeting with the chief executive, he wrote a blog post that included the meeting he had with me. He mentioned my book, *Daughter Arise*. It was a huge deal as the blog went to all the council employees. Some of my colleagues came and congratulated me, and I was touched by their lovely comments. On the same day his blog was released, he sent me a lovely email thanking me for loaning him the book, and no sooner had I received that email than the director of Children Services emailed me to ask if we could meet. Everything seemed to happen in quick succession, but it was all very positive.

The night before the meeting, I wrote down some of the jobs I thought I could do, such as a trainer. I created workshops and delivered them on behalf of Daughter Arise, and this was one of the services I planned to offer through my company, YEME Empowerment, that I was in the process of setting up. This made sense. It would kill two birds with one stone, so I thought. If I could get a job as a trainer, this would allow me to have a paid job with a stable monthly income that would please my husband and keep some financial stability. Also, it would keep my itchy feet still for a while whilst I developed my skills and built my company. This would keep me on track with my plans.

The meeting with the children's director went well. She seemed to take a genuine interest in what I had to say. She asked me questions about my journey and experience of being in care. I told her about some of the things I found difficult and shared with her the positive things I learned from going through such adverse circumstances. She asked about my TEDx talk and what the experience was like. The conversation flowed naturally, and I told her of my intention to hand in my notice. She expressed her surprise that I was going to leave and asked me what I was going to do. I told her I was going to set up a company that offers resources and services to facilitate the empowerment of people. I was surprised when she asked me not to act upon my intention to leave just yet. She asked me if I stayed what I wanted to do. I told her I wanted to be a trainer, and I asked her if there were any opportunities. She asked me what qualifications I had. As I prepared to answer her question, a wave of disappointment swept over me. I did not have an official qualification in training, but I had the experience of creating and delivering workshops for several years. I knew this type of job would be hard to get because usually, these jobs went to staff from a social work background, but I still took a chance to ask. At the end of the meeting, the director asked me to leave my request with her because she had to have a chat with someone to see if there were any options. To my surprise, she asked me if I would write a blog for her about child sexual exploitation to share my experience on this topic. I had a two-week deadline to write the post.

I was happy to receive such an incredible opportunity. As I excitedly left her office, I went to see a dear colleague of mine that I worked with, Caroline. Caroline was someone who was a support to me. She was one of only two people at work with whom I shared my recent developments. She was as excited as I was about my opportunity, and we both remarked how amazing it was to do something like this. I was naturally nervous because this was the director of the entire department that I worked for, but I knew I was up to the task—my four years of writing articles as a blogger prepared me for it.

I was proud of the article that I wrote, and in doing so, I realised there were many experiences from my life story that I had not yet shared that could be used to teach and empower others. When I was a teenager in care, I considered it a normal part of everyday life to go through challenging situations and circumstances. But in reflecting and looking back at my life during that time, the truth is, what I and other care-experienced people that were or are currently in care face is not normal. I tried to capture this through the blog I wrote and hoped that it would help professionals that work with young people to gain a different understanding of how circumstances in life can lead a young person into a vulnerable situation.

I emailed my blog article by the deadline, and I expected the process of publishing it to take some time. I anticipated the director might want me to make amendments, elaborate, or highlight certain points in more detail, but instead, she emailed and simply said thank you. It was a pleasant surprise. I don't know why but just like when I met with the chief executive, I had in my mind a preconceived notion that things would be difficult. That was another lesson learned during this process of stepping out of my comfort zone and taking risks; not to judge people or situations on first impressions. In my experience so far, I found the people deemed the most unapproachable because of their status or position were the most helpful.

I came to learn that I was the first person ever to write a blog post for the director. As news of my blog began to circulate around the organisation, it also marked another first. It was noted to be the most commented blog on her page. I was touched by the comments of colleagues that knew and didn't know me. Suddenly, I was thrust into a new light. People now knew about my book *Daughter Arise* and me. The director also recommended that people read my book. Over sixty staff brought my book. In between work, I was signing books and telling people in part about my journey. Many colleagues said I was an inspiration and that it was encouraging to see someone that came from the care system doing amazing things in life.

This period of my work life was amazing. How my journey started from a child that came into the care system in this borough to be the first person to write a blog for the current director of children's services was surreal. All these experiences continued to testify to me over and over again that God would turn what was meant for bad in my life into good. *"You intended to harm me, but God intended it for good to accomplish what is now being done, the saving of many lives"* **(Genesis 50:20).**

My life is proof that no matter where you start, regardless of background, it does not have to define your outcome. Some people were shocked and surprised that the director asked me to do a blog for her. This again showed me the organisational mindset that some people believed about certain opportunities only given to those in the clique or hierarchy. In other situations, I had seen and experienced this to be true. But not this time; God had shown me favour.

By the time I had my last meeting with the last person on my flow chart, the assistant director of children's services, I knew the door was well and truly closed at this employment. It was time to move on. The assistant director's words of encouragement during our meeting helped me to understand that what I had to offer was bigger than any position this organisation could offer me. I had a God-given purpose, and the work I was being led to do next was a calling, my purpose, not a career climbing move.

I had another confirmation in February 2018. After these meetings, as I was sleeping one night, I had a particularly significant dream. In the dream, a prophet, a man of God, came and said to me "to step out like Abraham." Abraham was a man in the Bible of great faith. As a matter of fact, he is described as the forefather of the Christian faith. He did many things in faith that included leaving behind all he had known to follow God to an unknown place. His faith in God was so strong that he was willing to sacrifice his son Isaac in obedience to God- even when he did not understand why. Abraham's story shows an example of what faith, trust, and obedience look like in action. My interpretation from the dream was that I also needed to start my journey of faith. The prophet in the dream told me that I was going to receive something life-changing during the journey. The next morning, I told my husband about the dream and that I was going to hand in my notice. This was the third confirmation I had received.

I think I needed to physically go through that 5-month process of meeting with the CEO, children director, assistant director, and head of service at my workplace to finally come to a conclusion and be at peace with myself that it was time to go. My aim of gaining a new work opportunity did not come to pass. Of course, if it was the will of God for me to stay, I would have (even though I would be upset), but it was not. I did not consider my time spent doing this exercise as a waste of time, as I got personal revelation on many things. It did not matter anymore whether they gave me an opportunity or not. I gained something far greater that I did not expect; the realisation that I had something within me that was bigger and more valuable than any position, title, or company. I became more convinced that within me, I held the answer to a specific problem, and through my gift of empowerment, I could help people find solutions to their problems. In my hand, I held the keys to unlock everything I wanted and desired to achieve. But I would have to leave my comfort zone to get it. There could be no safety net. It would personally cost me in some shape or form to pursue and achieve it. Without courage, faith, and risk, it would never be discovered. In March 2018, I handed in my notice. I left my job on 2nd April 2018. I took a deep breath and stepped into the unknown. I finally did it; I found the courage to leave.

CHAPTER THREE
INTO THE UNKNOWN

I dreamt about this moment for so long, and now that I was finally leaving my job, it felt unbelievable. I was excited and scared at the same time. This was my chance to discover what I was really made of. For the longest time, it seemed like a very distant dream, one that was unattainable. I always felt a tinge of sadness at the thought that I would not get a chance to do the things that I believed I was good at. I spent many days daydreaming, looking out of the bus window on the way to work, wondering how I could make my entrepreneur dream a reality. I thought I could make it work alongside my other commitments, but as time passed, it became clear; taking a risk was my only way forward. There was never going to be a perfect time. *If you wait for perfect conditions, you will never get anything done. (Ecclesiastes 11:4).* I had to take a chance. I was now forty-one years old. If I didn't act now, when would I? There was a risk if I waited any longer. I would miss an important opportunity. I decided to go for it despite my fears, insecurities, and not knowing the exact outcome. *Could I make it work? Was my self-belief and confidence in my abilities clouding my judgement? Was this a risk too far?* These were the questions I asked myself, and I still ask the same questions now.

I spent the first week after leaving my job resting and sleeping. I didn't realise how stressed and tired I was. In leaving my job, I felt a huge weight lifted off my shoulders. I was mentally free. I spent a huge part of my working life trying to fit into these work environments, and it made me miserable. I was not built for these places or the traditional nine to five work system. I felt bad that I struggled to fit in, and I always thought I was the problem. The unseen pressure to conform and fit in made me feel very uncomfortable. It was not an open requirement by any organisation I worked for; however, silently, this was the expectation. I never felt I could just be me and be accepted. This was important to me; to be true to myself. I felt like a square peg trying to fit into a round hole. Not any longer. I now had a chance to co-partner with God to create a different future, one that allowed me to do work that is meaningful.

In my excitement to get started, I overlooked how long it would take for me to start earning an income. I didn't know how long it would take because I hadn't done anything like this before. Fortunately for me, my ex-manager told me of an opportunity that would allow flexibility for me to gain an income whilst I worked on building my company. At first contractual work as an independent person (investigating children social care complaints) was slow coming in. It took a while for me to get established; however, things picked up. In the back of my mind, I thought, worst-case scenario, I could always get a part-time temping job if things became too hard. That is not what I wanted to do, but it was my subconscious plan B—part of the natural conditioning that came from working for others and comfort zone living.

But I have come to discover when you step out in faith with God, there is never a plan B. Only plan A; God's way.

For most of the last twenty-three years, I have always worked. There were only two short periods in my working life since the age of sixteen years old that I had not worked. The first time was when I left the government care system at seventeen years old. Besides being a single mum with my first flat, I had a lot of personal issues to contend with. I suffered from depression, and that made things difficult. My second stint of unemployment came years later when I left my job as an executive interview officer for the passport service. That period of unemployment lasted ten months before I got the job working as an administrator for the local authority that I was in care with as a child.

I felt strongly led to leave my job at the Home Office after five years of employment. The problem was I would not leave without another job in place. My mindset was very different then. At that point, I had not discovered my purpose or really developed the things I was good at. Also, my self-esteem and confidence were low. To leave a job without an income when I had financial commitments to take care of was a crazy idea. And the fear of not being able to pay my bills and help my family made me hesitant to leave.

But the decision to stay came at a cost. I had no peace, all for the sake of a paycheque. The stress and repetitive nature of the job proved to be the catalyst that pushed me to go after I came back from another period of sick leave. My husband was very supportive of my decision to leave and had a dream that I typed up my resignation letter. This was further confirmation for me as I also had a dream that I was in the ladies' room at work taking off my uniform shirt, remarking it had been a nice shirt. Six weeks later, I left. That was my first time stepping out of a job without another one in place to go to.

I did learn something very valuable from this experience. It helped me to recognise the signs when it was time to move on. Being able to discern these signs not only helped me in career decisions but in other life situations as well. Are you someone that recognises the signs that it's time to move on, but you feel stuck? I understand how that feels, especially when you have commitments and responsibilities to take care of. Maybe you are worried that you won't find another job like the one you have, or maybe you wonder how other people will view you if you do something different from what you are known for. Or do you believe that it's too late to pursue the things you dream of? Insecurities, fear, lack of confidence, or low self-belief will have you believing 'better the devil you know than the one you don't' or 'let me stick with what I know.' But please, believe me, the devil you know (your comfort zone) comes at a cost. You survive, not thrive. You remain unhappy and resent each passing day you stay stuck. How do I know? I have been there!

That crossroads moment comes to a head in one way or another. You may feel you have no choice, but contrary to belief, there is always a choice. It may not be a popular, easy, or comfortable choice, but there is choice, nevertheless. Either you find a way to free yourself from your situation or let it define you and your life. It is not an easy decision to make; it is downright hard. To leave the comfort of what you are used to, to embrace a journey of risk into the unknown goes against the very nature of how modern society and life we are conditioned to live. I cried and wrestled so many times with my decision to leave my job at the home office. I weighed up all the pros and cons. I prayed, fasted, and asked God if there was another way, an easier way to leave. I wanted a nicely prepared alternative that I could slot right into, like a pair of well-worn slippers. But it didn't happen like that. I had to step out, afraid, uncomfortable, and unsure of my decision.

It was hard for my family financially for me to leave my home office job. I prayed and continued to ask God for the next step. We had always been a two-income family on good salaries living to a good standard. It was hard for me to fathom being in such a position where I had no job, and pride did kick in. I was used to figuring things out and was self-reliant; I had to be. I learned from my time in care to be my own parent. I made my own decisions and lived life on my terms. This caused problems in the early years of my marriage and, of course, in my relationship with God because trust, co-dependence, and faith are the basis of our relationship.

I applied for a few jobs, and I got shortlisted for interviews. But it did not lead to me securing a job. I became very discouraged. I just wanted an income to help support my family. In between waiting for the right job opportunity to come up, I used the ten-month gap of unemployment to focus on and further develop my charitable organisation, Daughter Arise.

At the time, my husband's uncle was a consultant on my organisation, and he sent me information about a company that ran courses to help develop voluntary organisations. On visiting the website, I immediately saw a course on event management and fundraising that took my interest. Up until this point, I had only organised small events such as book launches and parties. I enjoyed doing them. On further reading about the course, I noticed there was a cost. It was expensive, and there was no way I could afford it. Since I left my job, I was living on less income than before whilst still covering the overheads of my charity. We were not getting any funding for running Daughter Arise, and my husband and I ran the organisation as volunteers. Paying for the course amid our financial downturn could be seen as a want, not a need or investment in the future. But I was looking at the bigger picture. This could be something that opened doors to new opportunities and could possibly create income. Besides, I would learn new skills. It was a bold move for me to apply, knowing I did not have all the money for it, but I chose to exercise faith and apply for the course anyway. As the saying goes, 'if you don't ask, you don't get.' If it was meant to be, a way would be open for me to be on the course.

I boldly typed the email and explained my circumstances. I told them why I wanted to do the course; that I wanted to learn how to host fundraising events to help people. I didn't wait long for a reply. To my surprise, I was offered a place on the three-day course that was taking place in Soho, London. I only had to pay twenty-five pounds (the course was £200.00). They made an exception because I was the director of a charitable organisation. I was shocked but gladly accepted the offer.

I wasted no time in putting what I learned on the course into action. In April 2013, I decided that I was going to put my newfound knowledge to the test by fundraising to host an event to raise awareness of childhood sexual abuse. I toyed with different theme ideas (gala, brunch, breakfast), but I eventually decided to do an afternoon tea event. Carefully I planned every detail and coupled with my previous experience, knowledge, and contacts, I began putting the event together. After working out the initial cost, I calculated that I needed to raise £850.00 pounds. The first person I approached was the pastor of my church. Excitedly I told him of my vision for the event and why I believed it would be successful. At first, his response was not what I had hoped for.

"Why would God want you to do such an event?" he inquired.

I simply responded to help those affected by sexual abuse. He couldn't believe that God would want me to do this, and I left the meeting feeling quite despondent. But in all fairness, my pastor was not the only person that thought I was crazy to attempt such a thing. Admittedly because of people's doubts and me not getting the support I thought I would get; I did go back and ask God several times if I was doing the right thing. I could see other people's viewpoints. It did seem like a crazy thing to be doing, especially when no one else had attempted a similar event (no one had at the time I checked the internet). The doubt even caused me to question if I was the right person to do it. *'Who am I?'* I thought to myself. *'Why would anyone come to an event to listen to me?* I was not a celebrity or a person that was even well known in my local community. But even with my doubts and insecurities, I still felt an impression that I was doing the right thing.

During the six months of planning, I experienced many tests and trials, both outward and inward. What I was trying to achieve, hosting an afternoon tea for a hundred people, felt like an impossible task at times. The only comfort and reassurance I had were that God was with me, and he showed me favour in all that I did. Churches, friends, and family that I approached for donations helped, and I had people come alongside me to support me with various tasks. I designed the programs on my laptop and approached organisations and people with different skills to support the event for free or at a discounted fee. I asked people that I knew to make cakes and got together a team of volunteers to help serve on the day. I accomplished the fundraising target with a few days to spare, and everything was booked and paid for. It was going well, but there was a problem. I still could not get the stands for the afternoon tea. With one day left until the event, it was not looking hopeful that I would get them. The stands were key to the event. Not only were they table centrepieces, but the entire theme was based on them. Without the stands, it would be glaringly obvious something was amiss.

It was not for the lack of effort on my behalf in trying to get them. I spent weeks in the lead up to the event contacting tableware hire companies to try and acquire the stands. This proved problematic, as the stands were either booked out, not the number of stands needed, or within the budget. I then decided to try and buy the stands. After searching the Internet for a considerable amount of time, I found one place, the day before the event, that had fourteen stands at a reasonable price; a store called Dunhelm. However, there was one small problem; the store was in Reading. By this point, I was tired and feeling slightly panicked. It was 11 am, and I would have to leave sharpish to get there. The store was an hour and thirty-minute train ride away, not including the bus ride to the train station. I felt like giving up at this point. How was I going to get there and back by 4.30 pm in time for my appointment at the jobcentre? I called Moureen, a colleague and friend of mine, to explain the situation. She was always someone that I could rely on for support. Moureen helped me to run the support group for two years as a volunteer and was one of my biggest supporters in the work I was doing with Daughter Arise. I listened with anticipation at her response to my dilemma, and I expected her to agree with me that this task was indeed impossible. Her response surprised me.

"Are you going to let this situation defeat you, Yvonne?" she asked.

"Well, look at the time and how far I have to go!" I replied.

"You need tea stands for the event, and if this is the only way you can get them well, you have to go. People are relying on you, and the event is tomorrow. You can do it."

She was right. I didn't want to do it but knew I had to. Her challenging words gave me the final push of motivation that I needed. All the tickets had sold, and people had contacted me inquiring if they could pay at the door. I could not let people down.

I dug out my small pink suitcase that I intended to use to carry back the tea stands from behind boxes under the stairs and set out on my journey. There was a plus side. The weather was unusually hot for September, way above the average temperature for this time of year. I arrived at the train station with a few minutes to spare to board my train. The journey was straightforward; however, on arriving at the other end, I had to take a bus to the store. I searched for the right bus stop, and I boarded the bus. Fortunately, the traffic was not too bad for a Friday afternoon. When I got off the bus, I could not find the store, so I asked a passer-by for directions. It turned out that Dunhelm was situated on an industrial estate, a 15-minute walk away. I was so tired from dragging the suitcase in the hot heat. It felt like the store was an hour away. I was drained of energy walking in the hot sun.

On entering the store, I was greeted by one of the customer advisers. I told her that I had reserved fourteen afternoon tea stands. She said she recognised my order, as she was the person I had spoken with on the phone earlier in the morning. As she went to get the stands, I browsed around the store. I didn't have to wait too long for her return. And as she approached me, I noticed the shopping trolley she was pushing was piled high with my order. I glanced at her trolley and then my tiny pink suitcase. I knew I had a problem; my case was too small. At that moment, I felt like bursting into tears, but I maintained my composure and explained my situation to her. The adviser told me to wait. I watched her go across the shop floor and return with a large suitcase from their display.

"*I want you to have this,*" she said.

"*What do you mean?* I replied

"*You have come from London to get these stands because you want to help others, and I want to help by giving this to you,*" she said.

"*I could not possibly take this from you,*" I exclaimed

But she was insistent. So, I gladly took her kind gift. I was truly touched by her gesture. I had never had something like this happen to me before. Her act of kindness energised me, and I soon forgot how tired I was. On leaving the store, she wished me luck with the event, and I thanked her again. Now with two suitcases in tow, I walked back to the bus stop to start my journey back to London. I arrived back at Clapham Junction station at 4.10 pm. I had twenty minutes to get to my appointment. I made it with five minutes to spare.

The Afternoon Tea event was a huge success. Moreover, it ran smoothly with no major setbacks. I was on a high for days after the event, and the feedback I received from the guests was amazing. The guests never knew of the challenges I encountered in getting the beautiful tea stands that served their delicious cakes and sandwiches. I was up at 6.00 am that morning buttering 17 loaves of bread. I had to cut off all the crusts and make the different fillings for the sandwiches. There were times before and during the event where I broke down crying because of the stress and pressure. But it was a small price to pay to see my vision come to pass. To see the survivors of child sexual abuse empowered and supported by people that cared was powerful. If I hadn't taken a risk, had the courage, and persevered, this wouldn't have been possible.

Even though I had doubts along the way, I was determined to succeed. Of course, people doubted my idea, but I have come to find that it is a normal part of the journey when you pursue something you believe in. Taking the journey into the unknown will require you to push through your circumstances to find a way to overcome the obstacles that block your opportunities. You cannot let doubters, haters, or naysayers get in your way. It is important to hold onto your dream and believe in it when no one else does. Had I focused on my temporary circumstances, challenges, or my lack of confidence, I probably would not have picked up the phone to inquire about the course. I'm glad I did, and as they say, the rest is history.

Well, not quite history. Because here I was five years later in what appeared to be an identical situation. Apart from the fact, I had again stepped out of a job without another one in place that resulted in a period of financial struggles is where the similarities end. There were major differences between now and then. Five years before, when I was at the home office, I was healing from a few devastating things that affected me quite deeply. But I overcame them, and they no longer affected the way I saw my life or me. There is a saying that goes, 'what does not break you makes you stronger.' In terms of the challenges I faced at different points in my life, I have found this saying to be true. Going through various seasons of adversity built my character and made me more resilient. Trials, tests, and challenges led me to have a deeper understanding of who I was and helped me to discover my purpose and calling. My mindset changed as I grew in confidence, and so did my perspective on life. I no longer believed situations like stepping out of a job would be the end for me. I knew leaving my job at Wandsworth was for a particular purpose. That's it. The major difference was I discovered my purpose. The journey then and now, is difficult but understanding it's part of a bigger plan makes it bearable. Transition is a hard and difficult process. However, making choices is the bridge I had to cross to have a revelation about these things. The journey between then and now was a time of personal transformation—a time to break away from all that had kept me captive emotionally, mentally, and spiritually.

"Behold God is doing a new thing; do you not perceive it?" **(Isaiah 43:19)** The signs of a 'new thing' were given to me in a word of prophecy from God through Pastor Eric in April 2017 during a prayer meeting I was attending at Phoebe Academy. God shared through him that it was time for me to leave my job at Wandsworth. And that the next time I go back there, it would be in a different capacity. This was further confirmation it was time to leave. The prophecy came to pass in April 2018 when three

weeks after I left my job, I was booked as a guest speaker at a training event for social workers, foster caregivers, and other professionals at Wandsworth. Not only was I sharing my past experiences to empower and give insight to staff that look after children in care, but the training facility where it was held was at the school that I left twenty-eight years earlier. I was expelled from Burntwood School because of my unmanageable behaviour that stemmed from the trauma of my abuse. I left that school at fourteen years old at the beginning of my journey in care. It was a full-circle moment for me as I stood in that classroom. It was profound and emotional. I had tasted the promise of a new thing. I knew God was doing something different in my life, but I was not clear exactly what it was.

Exactly four weeks after leaving my job at Wandsworth and one week after taking part in the event, I was admitted to the hospital for an emergency operation. Afterwards, I was unable to do anything for six weeks. I was in bed on painkillers, and I could hardly walk down the stairs, let alone leave the house. The reality of our financial situation was at the forefront of my mind each day. I worried about the impact this sudden health crisis would have on my family and finances. I was frustrated and became quite down; this was not where I imagined myself to be. My entrepreneur journey got off to the worst start possible.

Being confined to bed left me with too much time to focus on the negative aspects of my situation. I started to feel insecure about myself, and things were not going well in my marriage. But I still felt a strong conviction that despite the difficulties, it was the right decision to leave my job. I spent many sunrises on my knees on my office floor, crying to God for help and strength. I also found it difficult to be dependent on my husband financially because I had always paid my way. I felt I had no right to ask him for money. As a matter of fact, I was very uncomfortable doing so. But I trusted God to provide, and He did in many ways. I came to know God personally during this period of my life as El-Shaddai (God is my provider). There was no room for pride, only faith, and humility. When I was at my lowest, God was there with me.

CHAPTER FOUR
DOORS OF OPPORTUNITY

I was casually scrolling on Twitter (social media app) one afternoon when I saw a re-tweet (that is when someone reposts a comment) by the ex-director of children's services (from my old workplace). The tweet was about an opportunity to get free training to become a qualified trainer. I was excited to see this tweet because I did not have a recognised qualification even though I designed and delivered my own workshops over the years. Immediately I clicked on the link attached to the tweet. On further investigation, I realised there were limited spaces available on the course as it was a one-time opportunity. There were two conditions to apply. Firstly, I had to have connections with the borough of Wandsworth (which I did through my work with Daughter Arise), and I had to write and submit a short statement on why I wanted to do the course. I wasted no time in applying. If my application were successful, I would find out in six weeks' time.

It was now July 2018, and I was back on my feet after my operation. It took me a while to gain my strength back, but day by day, with exercise, I got better. It was also the month I officially started work as a self–employed person. Most of my work came from contracts, one on one training, and consultancy work. I was also commissioned by my old employer to do their annual social events. It was a blessing to be given these contracts. And it started to dawn on me that there was a lot to learn in my new career as an entrepreneur. Fortunately for me, I had a good foundation of discipline and skills that I acquired during my years in traditional paid employment that served me well. I adjusted to some things with ease.

I worked hard and long hours to honour all the work I was contracted to do. But I did not mind. What I love about being an entrepreneur is the variation of work; no two days are the same. Some days I am planning for an event; other days advising people on charitable organisation start-ups. Some afternoons I spend creating workshops or visiting bookstores to introduce my books. This is what I wanted. And it was a world away from sitting at a desk undervalued, letting life pass me by. Stephen, my husband, always commented that I was never cut out for office environments, and he was right. Even with the financial challenges and wondering where to find new contacts, I was optimistic about my future. I was confident that my skills, talents, and experiences would take me far and be of great benefit to others and that in due time I would reap the financial rewards. I believed I could make my business work.

I was delighted to find out that I was accepted on the training course. I also found out the reason why it was the last time the course would be offered, and the European Union would no longer fund it. It was another one of those intriguing moments where I could see the hand of God orchestrating my path. I mean, what are the chances of how this opportunity came about? I had met with the director of the children's service at my last employment four months earlier about possibly becoming a trainer, only to find no jobs available. I leave to start my own company. I see a tweet from the same director about an opportunity to train as a trainer. I applied and got offered a place. Go figure.

The course was every Wednesday for twelve weeks, and I thoroughly enjoyed doing it. I learned so much about the theory behind becoming a trainer, such as how to develop structured training to deliver the best possible learning outcomes for students. To get the qualification, I had to complete assignments every week. As part of the requirements, I had to deliver a training session to my classmates as part of the assessment. Sometimes it was a challenge to juggle studying with all my other responsibilities, but I pushed through. All my hard work and determination paid off in the end; I passed my assessment. As a result, I became a qualified trainer.

This opportunity for free training led to other great doors of opportunity opening for me. The training department of my old employer commissioned me to deliver workshops to social workers and professionals. This was the same department I had hoped to get a job in when I met with the director of children's services at the time.

I could never imagine that things would work out this way, but it was for the best. Because instead of being pigeonholed in one job role, through the services I offered with my company YEME Empowerment I had the freedom to do other things too. The prophecy Pastor Eric gave me the previous year about going back to my previous employer had come to pass in more ways than one as I was hired for various contracts with them.

Opportunities continued to spring up from different places; some apparent others were not. For example, eight months after my TEDx talk launched on YouTube, a lady from California contacted me. This itself was nothing new. Since the TEDx talk, I have received emails from survivors in different parts of the world. People got in touch to tell me that my speech had inspired them. It was encouraging to know that my talk had made an impact on their life.

The lady from California was a survivor of sexual abuse. On watching my video, she explained it was the first time she had seen someone clearly articulate the challenges she was currently facing.

From the tone of her email, I could sense her urgency in needing help. She had contacted me through YEME Empowerment, my business, not Daughter Arise, my charitable organisation, inquiring about empowerment coaching, as she wanted help to change her life. She did not have much money but was willing to pay for this service. I decided to help her for free.

Over six months, on Sunday evenings, we would Skype call. Because of the time difference between California and London, I would talk with her at 10:00 pm. This meant I would go to bed late and be tired the next day, but I didn't mind. Because I could see how much these sessions meant to her and the changes she was making, it was worth it. At the end of each call, I would give her something positive to work on and pray with her.

Celina's life experiences caused her to isolate from people. I could totally understand why. To go through childhood sexual abuse is one of the worst betrayals a child can experience, and often it comes at the hands of someone the child knows, loves, and trusts.

Celina was such an endearing lady. Throughout our sessions, I saw a change in her demeanour. She was optimistic about her future and had started to connect with people again. Her hopelessness and despair began to dissipate, and instead, she sensed there was hope for her future. Our sessions helped her not to focus on her abuse but on the potential of what she could become and her future goals. Celina said no one had ever told her the things I had before regarding sexual abuse. Because of this, the perception she once held about herself changed. I was amazed to see how my personal experience and knowledge could influence and impact someone so profoundly. I can honestly say Celina was not the only one that benefited from our talks.

Speaking with her and witnessing her mental and spiritual transformation provided moments of epiphany for me. I realised the power of the calling God gave me to empower people. I underestimated the value of my lived experience and the knowledge I gained in understanding my own pain. How blessed was I not only to have survived but thrived from adversity! Our talks gave me a renewed sense of confidence in my authority to speak on such things.

Out of the blue, during one of our sessions, Celina asked me if I would consider coming to

California to host an event for survivors. Celina was inspired not only because of the support she received from me but also by the work I was doing in England to support survivors. She was convinced others would appreciate my knowledge and asked me to think about it whilst she was away. Celina was moving to another state and would not be in contact for a couple of months. On her return, should I agree to her request, we would start work immediately on planning the event.

I told Celina I would think about it. But in my head, I had already decided to say no. I mean, why would I fly across the other side of the world, to a place I had never been before, where no one knows me to hold an event? I was sure it was a bad idea. I spoke with my mentor Cheryl about it. And she thought it was a great idea.

"How could this be a good idea?" I asked.

"A prophet is never appreciated in their own town," Cheryl replied.

I understood what she was saying. Not that I was literally a prophet or that I ever considered myself to be one. She was talking about all I had to offer being rejected over here (in London). Jesus was not accepted in His hometown when He was doing miracles amongst His own people. His work could not have the impact it was supposed to because of their unbelief. People looked at His family background and his given occupation and dismissed Him. *"Is this Jesus the carpenter? Joseph's son?" they asked incredulously (***Luke 4:14-30***).* I found I could relate to aspects of Jesus's experience.

Over the last decade, I tried every avenue to share my knowledge and expertise, but people in certain circles did not value or appreciate it. I tried the perceived 'right way,' and it got me nowhere. But I didn't let that stop me. I created my own opportunities. I wrote two books about childhood sexual abuse. I have done a TEDx talk, put on my own events, and have been a public speaker. I did a presentation before elected members- The Mayor of Lambeth, council leaders, and councillors at a deputation meeting. I met with CEOs, applied for a consultancy post with the Independent Inquiry into Child Sexual Abuse. I emailed organisations, churches, called schools to introduce my workshops. I asked for my organisation, Daughter Arise, to be listed as a resource for residents in my local community. And I offered to be a people champion on sexual abuse within my borough, but I was turned down. I knocked on lots of doors of perceived opportunity, but many of them were locked. They did not like my message and did not accept the messenger. My message and my proven ideas for empowering those affected fell on deaf ears.

Few prominent people were willing to support or help me. I never once claimed to know it all; I just knew what helped me overcome challenges in my life and the lives of others that I supported. Often, I was looked upon as "less than," and my knowledge was deemed non-valid because I did not have an excellent educational background. Education is important, but would a degree make a difference to those in need of hope? I think not. People that find hope are empowered by others that have come through similar experiences. People told me many times I had no right to do certain things because I did not have certain accolades. But it is God who decides at His discretion whom He chooses to make great. *"He uses the things considered foolish by the world to confound the wise"* **(1 Corinthians 1:27).**

There were other reasons why people in these circles felt unease about me. I was perceived as being very religious because I confess through my life testimony that I am a follower of Christ. Yes, I am a Christian. I am a woman of God, and I am not ashamed of that. The love and freedom I found through Jesus are what I try and show to others through my actions. As a matter of fact, I wish I were bolder in my faith because I was rejected anyway.

Judgements were also made about me because of my past. This served many people well over the years whose intentions were to try and destroy me. I was not supposed to be living life this well as someone that came from my background (the care system and a survivor of childhood sexual abuse). I was supposed to just survive, not to thrive, embittered about the hand life dealt me, but I am not. I also sensed stereotypes about me based upon the colour of my skin as well. It was something I never noticed until I started trying to make something of myself.

Challenges and rejection are not new to me it is something I have known my whole life. Even though knockbacks have left me discouraged at times, I bounce back because I am resilient. I focus on the vision, purpose, and calling God gave me to empower people that want positive life change. Labels will never define me, and adversity has trained me well. People with low expectations of me had better get used to seeing me exceed because I will continue to arise with God. As Cheryl mentioned, elsewhere in the world, what I have to offer is an answer to prayer.

One of the business goals that I set out before I launched my company was to do an empowerment event abroad. My company YEME Empowerment offers training, resources, and services to facilitate the empowerment of people. It encompasses everything I am experienced, talented, and skilled at. I thought doing an international event would be possible in three to five years. I believed an opportunity like this would come about after I marketed my company tirelessly to gain exposure and attend endless networking events to connect with the right people. Only when I was more established did I believe that opportunities like this would be available to me. I envisioned it to be a slow progression rather than a quick succession. Once again, through Celina's request, I was reminded that God's way is different from man's way.

I decided to host an event in California after my talk with Cheryl and much prayer and consideration. I never received a big 'yes' written in the sky from God as confirmation that it was the right decision. In my experience, answer to prayer never happens like that. Instead, I decided to view it as an opportunity. I had nothing to lose in trying, and it was something different.

How many times had I prayed the prayer of Jabez? *"Oh, God would bless me and enlarge my territory?"* **(1 Chronicles 4:10***).* I wanted to do great and mighty things. I wanted an adventure. This would either be one of the most amazing things I have ever done in my life or a big mistake. What I had learned from all my life experiences this far that called me to go beyond my reasoning and understanding is there always is something to learn or gain from taking risks. Sometimes not in the way I necessarily expected either. A sense of peace would have to be my confirmation in going forward. I was willing to walk the tightrope of courage once again.

CHAPTER FIVE

ENLARGE THE TENT

No sooner had Celina settled in from her move to another state in Los Angeles, she contacted me. It was then I told her of my decision to do the event. Celina was so excited. So was I because I had never done anything like this.

Before her move, Celina had sent me pictures of an event she had done when she worked for the police federation. The event was held on a moored boat on a lovely summers evening. The décor was beautiful; flowers and tea lights adorned the main room. Against the dark night sky, the ship looked magical. I could tell by looking at the pictures that the guests enjoyed themselves. I felt reassured when I looked at the pictures that together, we would create a memorable and well-planned event. With our combined skills and experience, we would make it work.

The Sunday evenings that I spent over the previous six months supporting and praying with Celina became our time to brainstorm and plan the event. I can admit I felt completely out of my depth, if I am honest, a little scared. It felt like I was playing a game of blind man bluff (a game I used to play as a kid where you are blindfolded, and another person guides you in the direction you need to go). It just so happened, in this case, I was the one having to exercise blind faith and trust God for guidance whilst working with someone I did not know. Nevertheless, it was exciting and nerve-racking at the same time. I likened this feeling I had in my stomach to riding on a rollercoaster. I imagined it must be similar. I have never been on one. As I suffer from motion sickness, I would never dare to go on one!

Because of work commitments and the time difference between our respective countries, we agreed to keep in touch by email, in-between our once-a-week Sunday phone call. One of the first things we decided on straight away was to set the date to hold the event. We agreed on 25th May 2019. It was now November 2019, six months until the big day. In my experience, this was long enough to plan an event. From that moment, I started to plan the concept and other details regarding it. It took Celina and me a month to discuss and research the basics. We made great strides in progress.

Celina, unbeknownst to me, wrote a letter to Ellen DeGeneres, a well-known talk show host in America. Her show is watched by millions of people worldwide. Celina told me about the letter a couple of weeks later. When she emailed me a copy of the letter, I cried. No one had ever written a letter on my behalf before, let alone one so heartfelt. The letter was passionate and supportive of the work I had done.

What Celina had seen in me through our interactions was something that continued to amaze me. I never considered what I was doing a big deal. I guess because it was in my nature to help people. I remember someone once shared whilst praying for me a vision of me being a ship on the ocean. The person painted a picture that as the ship travelled, it left a white foam trail as it went, meaning that as I went from place to place sharing my story, this signified the impact of my testimony and the hope I gave to others. It was a beautiful picture. I understood at that moment that what I did for others was never meant for me to value or understand; it was to encourage them.

Ellen never replied to the letter Celina wrote. It would have been a lovely surprise if she did. Nevertheless, the gesture was appreciated. As a reminder of the wonderful thing she had done, I kept a copy of the letter and placed it with my other cherished keepsakes of notes, cards, and letters I received over the years in a scrapbook that I made.

Celina was not put off from having no response from Ellen. She decided it would be a good idea to contact other celebrities in California to tell them about the event to ask if they would donate. This aspect of event planning was totally new to me, but it was great to learn about it. Celina told me American people responded positively to charitable causes and to those that do the work. I was willing to give her suggestion a try and trusted her guidance. After all, I knew nothing about American culture or what Californian people would respond well to. We made a list of celebrities to contact that we thought might be interested in supporting survivors of child sexual abuse and molestation (this is what they call sexual abuse in the states) and contacted them.

During this time, the Me Too movement received global media interest. It was a talking point across the world as victims of sexual assault and harassment came together to unite. Famous celebrities such as Michael Jackson, Robert Kelly (R.Kelly), Bill Cosby, and Harvey Weinstein were in the media spotlight for various alleged indiscretions and abuse. The solidarity amongst the victims that came forward to allege sexual harassment and abuse against certain celebrities became known as Me Too.

The Me Too movement was not a new phenomenon. Tarana Burke, a sexual harassment survivor, and activist started it on the social media platform, Myspace in 2006. It has become a powerful collective motivation for other social justice groups and empowerment movements to come together. Survivors of childhood sexual abuse also united and found solidarity in sharing a public voice through the Me Too movement.

Not everyone was pleased. Certain groups within society hated the movement. They called it divisive, an instigator for women to make up slanderous lies and accusations. Even with the outcry from certain quarters, it still received positive press because it provided a platform for people that otherwise would never have the courage to speak out. On seeing first-hand the positive effect it had on survivors, I decided to name the event Empower. The reason for this is because we wanted to empower survivors through social interaction, awareness, and education to find their voice. I had witnessed many times through events I created that peer empowerment is a powerful tool in providing hope and creating change.

Finding a venue proved tricky to begin with. It was hard for me to know what was available in California, as I lived on the other side of the world. Celina suggested that we look at vineyards, and she sent me brochures to look at. At first glance, it seemed like a good idea, but there were a couple of problems with holding the event at a vineyard. Firstly, the event premises served alcohol. Because of the type of guests attending, I did not want to put anyone in a vulnerable position. Secondly, the amount of money needed to hire the venue was expensive. There was no way we could raise 7,000 pounds in such a short space of time. Instead, I did a Google search for venues. We contacted church halls and community theatres but to no avail. They did not have all the amenities needed for the event.

It took us a while to find the perfect venue, and we found it right in the heart of Rancho Cucamonga, California. It was a community centre leased by the county (the equivalent of a borough Council in the U.K). They had several community centres based around their central park. Lions Centre West was set in a beautiful location. Palm trees gloriously lined the pavements leading to its entrance. It looked picture risqué with the bright shining sun accentuating the beauty of its surroundings. Besides being in a lovely location, it had all the amenities we required apart from a PA system. This was not a big deal as we could hire it separately. Without hesitation, Celina paid the deposit to secure the date because the venue was getting booked quickly. She scanned the paperwork and sent it to me. Once I completed it and submitted a proposal, everything was confirmed.

My next task was to find organisations to present at the Empower event. I was surprised at the number of non-profits that supported victims and survivors of Childhood Sexual Abuse in California. Just looking at all the information available, it was clear the issue was taken seriously. I needed two organisations. One to present on how sexual abuse affects adult survivors in the aftermath, and another organisation to educate on warning signs to look out for in children of possible sexual abuse. Within two weeks, we secured the first organisation. San Bernardino Sexual Assault Services agreed to come and present on the issues faced by adult survivors in the aftermath. Finding an organisation to present information on warning signs of sexual abuse in children took a while longer.

God works in mysterious ways. I mentioned the problem I was having in finding such an organisation to a lady that attended the monthly support group that I ran. She is American, and it just so happened that she went to university near Rancho Cucamonga and knew of the work organisations based there. She suggested Project Sister. Project Sister is an organisation that raises awareness of sexual abuse within the family environment and works tirelessly as a voice for children. I contacted them the next day.

I thought it would be a hard task to get organisations to agree to be a part of the event. In emailing both organisations, I was honest and upfront about what I could offer them in return for their time. I could only cover travel costs, supply lunch for the volunteers, and a stand for them to promote their work. It boosted my morale that despite what was on offer, both organisations wanted to support the cause. To ensure communication of any updates about the event, I officially appointed Celina as the event liaison coordinator to deal with any queries from our partners in California.

To estimate the cost of putting the event together, Celina and I acquired three quotes for each item needed. This allowed me to come up with an overall amount that we needed to fundraise for. I worked out that we would need £2,800 to cover the event cost. This did not take into consideration my plane ticket or accommodation. However, I was pleasantly surprised when Celina offered to let me use one of her company cabins during my stay without charge. The pictures of the cabin looked lovely, and it was a wonderful gesture, typical of her thoughtfulness. I accepted her offer. After the event, she promised to take my daughter and me sightseeing. My Daughter, Jada, was so excited as she wanted to see Hollywood and visit an American mall. I was not bothered. I was just excited at the prospect of hosting my first event abroad. Having the accommodation sorted out was a weight off my mind as I was still trying to figure out how I cover the extra cost on top of my family outgoings. I had only been self-employed for seven months and on less income than I was in part-time employment. I was not complaining, though. This was part and parcel of stepping into the unknown to start a business as an entrepreneur.

Between us, Celina and I devised a strategy to fundraise the money. Out of all aspects of charitable event planning, fundraising was my least favourite part. I always felt uncomfortable asking people for money. I felt like I was begging or harassing people. I hated it but understood it as a means to an aim. I set up a GoFundMe page and promoted it across all my social media platforms. I sent text messages and emails to people I knew. Celina decided on a personal approach, writing a letter to wealthy clients in her company to ask for donations. She put a lot of thought into her idea and brought beautiful note-writing paper and envelopes for the letters. We worked together on a power-point presentation. This was for Celina to present to the clients at her company. It provided information about the charitable work I had done over the years and the background of who I was.

Celina's Boss donated $150.00. He was the first official donor of the event and he also offered his company as one of the event sponsors. This was fantastic news as it meant we now had transportation for equipment and goods and a donation towards the food. We intended to cater for 120 people.

I also decided to ticket the event. This was for two reasons. Firstly, it would allow funds to be raised towards the cost. And secondly, it would encourage potential guests that this was a worthwhile event to attend. In my experience, doing events for free never seemed to attract the commitment of serious attendees. The ticket price was a reasonable $10.00. This included lunch, entertainment, access to great speakers, and resources.

We worked ridiculously hard to make this event a reality because we both believed it would encourage and help many people. We sent emails to churches in Rancho Cucamonga to inform them of the upcoming event and to ask for volunteers to serve the guests. At first, I was quite adamant that the church should provide volunteers. But with no churches responding to our emails, Celina suggested her work colleagues as an alternative. It took me a short while to come around to the idea. But with time running out, it was the best decision.

There were other priorities to focus on. We emailed local media in California to ask if they would do a story on what we were doing. We emailed companies such as Walmart and Costco to ask for food contributions. I emailed Gayle King, Tyler Perry, tweeted Oprah Winfrey and other well-known public figures for support. Because they had disclosed in the media, they were survivors of childhood sexual abuse. We would have been happy with a tweet or some type of acknowledgement. I had hoped the continuous media coverage of the Me Too movement and the breaking news stories surrounding it would work to our advantage. It did not. No one contacted us back.

Even though Celina and I were initially disappointed, it did not dampen our determination to see the event become a reality. Celina and I saw this as more than an event. We saw it as an opportunity to potentially save lives, in addition to providing hope to other people that had similar experiences to us. I have always been a passionate and determined person. When I set my mind to do something, I focus on doing it. Even when the odds are against me, the reassurance of God, His strength, and confidence in me encourage me to go forward. Even in times when I am scared and do not know what to do.

Passion for the vision is the fuel that keeps me going when I want to give up. It is the same passion that I had thirteen years ago to empower those that felt they had no voice. My God-given gift of empowerment goes way beyond the ability to help those affected by abuse; my experiences and the different life challenges I have overcome since then. I have been blessed with the unique ability to use my life experiences to empower and inspire people from all walks of life that are facing certain challenges.

I shared with Celina the vision I had for my empowerment work and the potential I saw for the future. From what I described, she was able to envision it too and was excited and enthusiastic about it. From our conversations, Los Angeles possibly seemed like a place where my empowerment work could thrive. My Mentor Cheryl also confirmed that America is a place where dreams are encouraged. I got the impression this was a place that embraced people with an entrepreneurial spirit to explore their ideas without prejudice and stereotypes because of their background. This sparked an interest in me to further explore this as a possible option in the future.

As the donations trickled in, I paid for things for the event. With the first twenty-five pounds raised, I hired a graphic designer to create a flyer for the event. He came up with a powerful image, and I was pleased with the design. Once it was completed, I posted it across different social events and media platforms in London and California. To get physical copies of the flyer to California would have been costly as I was based in England, and I could not process the order on my end. Instead, I guided Celina on how to do it from California. I believed 500 flyers would be enough to promote an event for 120 people, but Celina suggested we print 1,000 flyers. I was concerned about the pressure this would put on her to distribute them. She was already working long hours, and to deliver the flyers would mean her doing it on her day off. The task was further complicated because she lived two hours from Rancho Cucamonga, where the event would be held. She was adamant this would not be a problem. On one occasion, she drove all the way to Rancho Cucamonga only to find she had forgotten to pack the flyers in her car. She had to go back later that week. I felt bad for her.

Everything was proving costly with the event. As the weeks progressed, we had to re-think some of our initial plans. For instance, we wanted to hire a caterer to take care of the sandwiches, cakes, and sides for the event. It was now February, and set fundraising targets were not met. Celina suggested we buy platters of sandwiches, drinks, cakes, and crisps from Costco. That was a funny conversation. I spent quite a bit of time explaining to Celina what crisps are, only to find out in America they are called potato chips! Lunch was called luncheon. There were trans-Atlantic pronouns and interpretations we had to navigate, but those moments provided much-needed laughter.

Apart from the donations from Celina's boss and people that knew me, we were yet to make a dent in the fundraising target. For all my efforts in posting the event on social media, I only raised £50.00 via these platforms. Child sexual abuse is a hard cause to raise money for. The fact it was being held abroad didn't readily persuade people to give either. I had a few comments from people because the event was taking place in California. It seemed to put certain people off donating as they viewed it as an idyllic place to holiday, not somewhere to go and raise awareness of a worthwhile cause. California is known as the sunshine state *(as mentioned by Dr. Dre and Tupac in their song California Love-remix, one of my favourite songs)*. And yes, I admit California does conjure up images of palm trees and sunny days. But as I clarified a few times, I was not going for a holiday but as a volunteer to work. Despite having to battle through the challenges, awareness of this issue is needed. Sexual abuse does not always leave physical scars. Most of the time, it is the psychological scars that leave a long-lasting impact. It has always been hard for people to understand this. But Celina and I soldered on grateful for the people that did support us in what we were doing.

Good news came at the time when I most needed it. One day out of the blue, an acquaintance contacted me. She offered to pay for me and my family's plane ticket to California. She explained that as she was praying, God told her to make this offer. I was shocked. It was totally out of the blue. I had planned on buying our tickets and never expected anyone to pay for me. She said it was a gift from her to my family, but my husband did not want to go. Later that week, I booked the plane tickets for my daughter and me. Yet again, I was reminded that where God guides, He provides. God blessed me most unexpectedly, and this was further confirmation that He called me to do this event. Imagine, I did not have to pay for my own ticket! God sorted it out. That is the amazing thing about God. When He calls you to do something, He will make a way for His plan to come to pass. Now I was definitely going. But why did I still have moments of doubt?

The reason I believe I was having doubts was because of the nature of the 'ask' and the size of the 'task.' This event completely took me outside of my comfort zone. It tested my capabilities, my resources, understanding, capacity, and strength.

God had indeed enlarged my tent into an unknown place. Not having anyone around me that had attempted a similar feat before made me think it was an odd and wrong thing to do.

This made perfect sense. Because we are mostly conditioned to think, in society, that if everyone is doing it, then it is the right thing to do. Yet the people God used throughout history that made the most impact did things no one else was doing, and they were courageous. Jesus was the ultimate example of this. I learned that if you want to be comfortable and fit in with the crowd, you will do nothing that is remembered; it is courage that stands the test of time. It is understandable why many people choose not to do radical things. It is hard. To step into the unknown is a risk, and the likelihood of adversity comes with it. No wonder many people would rather avoid it. To attempt something like what I was doing requires that you give it your all. Every day was a challenge for me to push past fear and have complete faith and trust in God. Only time would tell if the things I have done in my life would be remembered.

I spent a lot of my time in prayer to God for help and encouragement. So many times over the last few months, I felt overwhelmed. My journey into the unknown was difficult. Even with the support of a couple of friends, I still felt alone. This feeling of loneliness was not in a physical sense. I felt alone because I knew no one that had undertaken something like what I was about to embark on. The closest thing I had for comfort and reassurance was Jackie Pullingers book *Chasing the Dragon*. As I read it for the third time, I felt a deep connection and understanding with the emotions and questions Jackie had about her own unknown journey. That feeling of being out of depth and not knowing what was around the corner was emotionally draining at times. Even so, despite my feelings, the courage to be bold in the face of the impossible is what was required. In reading her book, I understood I was not weird or odd in what I felt. As Jackie so eloquently explained, this was a part of the rollercoaster journey of being called into the unknown. Her book gave me the encouragement to keep going.

My choice to keep going and follow God continued to cause problems in my marriage. God told my husband to support me in what He called me to do, but he found it challenging. Part of him wanted to, but on the other hand, he was insistent that I should get a proper job (back in traditional employment as a temp). He did not think I was using common sense. It was hard for me to continuously explain that this is what I was called to do and that I was walking by faith. Do not get me wrong. I understood his concerns. I had them too. Even though I had contracted work, it was not as much as I would have had liked, so in a moment of panic, I did sign up with job agencies. Not because I didn't believe I was doing the right thing. It was because I felt pressure and a bit of failure for not bringing in enough money. And, of course, I did not want my husband to continue to be upset. In the end, I didn't follow through with job applications with the agencies. I decided to continue to trust God.

Some of you reading this book may think I am a complete madwoman. You may be wondering why God would want me to trust Him to provide for my needs when I am perfectly capable of getting a job, especially when faced with the possibility that any day real financial hardship could come knocking at the door. All I can say is that my relationship with God is based on faith, trust, and obedience. Therefore, if God has asked me to do something, I must trust Him and do it. What I was doing was not about me, even though I was the one undertaking the journey. I had to put my money where my mouth is, so to speak. How could I confess to trust God and not trust His plan for my life? Some things I have come to understand in life are more than my own needs and wants and even more than what my husband wants.

I sometimes wondered whether I was selfish in my single-minded pursuit and focus on following the call of God when faced with the unhappiness of my husband. Was I stupid to trust God for an outcome of something that I could not physically see based upon His promises to me? After all, my husband was carrying the brunt of the financial burden since I became self-employed. There were months when my income was sporadic. I felt the weight of my choice in his lack of affection towards me. There were times I felt I deserved it, even though I did not. Some things are hard to understand unless you are living them. But the situation called for understanding and patience on both sides. Whilst I believed I was doing the right thing, I had to understand that my husband may never embrace or agree with my decision. I also had to understand he only wanted the best for our family. He felt like the hopes and dreams for our family were slipping away because of my actions. And he had to understand that my love for God and desire to put Him first through my obedience to His call was important to me. We both wanted the same things. It is just the route in getting it we saw differently. This is where faith and common sense collided. It took some time for me to stop feeling guilty about my decision even though I had peace about it. I took comfort in the fact that God was with me in the situation. I knew the true intentions of my heart. I was not a heartless or irresponsible person, far from it. I decided to carry on walking forward, trusting and hoping that it would turn out okay in the end.

I expressed my darkest fears of failure and the pressure of my circumstances to my mentor Cheryl. Over the course of our sessions, I realised yet again there would be a high price to pay for following the call of God. I always understood there was a cost for going against the things considered normal. So, I don't know why I expected this situation to be different from other times in my life. Time and time again, I paid the price to stand for truth, to live the life I have today.

I had conversations with other Christians about the price of faith and the cost of following God. I was interested to hear their thoughts. I was shocked to hear Christians who profess to be followers of Jesus tell me that I should use common sense. It seemed for some having faith and putting it into action were two different things. Yet, when I read my Bible, it clearly tells me that "*without faith, it is impossible to please God*" **(Hebrews 11:6).**

In some of our discussions, Cheryl and I talked about whether the demands of living in society today made it impossible for modern-day Christians to live by faith. Was it possible to totally rely on God like Moses, Elisha, and Joshua? Ordinary people used by God to do great exploits. I had my doubts at times, especially when I was trying to live according to my faith, only to be told to use common sense. I did, however, take comfort in a story my mentor Cheryl shared with me about the time she pursued a dream she had. She was in a music group with three other ladies. They were offered a recording contract that opened an opportunity to go to America. It was her big break, one that she and the other ladies in the group waited a long time for, but it came at a cost. It appeared that Cheryl would have to give up her secure (and good) job to pursue the opportunity. After much prayer, she decided to take a chance and go for it. Cheryl told her manager of her decision. To her surprise, her employer offered her a career break and kept her job open for her until she returned. Cheryl was prepared to risk it all for her dream, and God honoured that. She understood that some opportunities only come around once in a lifetime and that when it does you have to be prepared to take a risk. Even though that dream was for a season in her life, she had no regrets, only great memories.

I wanted to experience the same thing. I wanted a great adventure. For most of my life, I had gone along with the expected and comfortable thing to do. For so long, until my early thirties, the aftermath of my abuse and other situations caused by people meant I spent a lot of time dealing with the consequences of their actions and mine. I followed wherever the course of those decisions led me, whether good or bad. It was through the rough and rugged journey of healing and self-discovery that I found my identity and purpose. I realised my potential, and I dared to believe and want more from my life. With courage, I had experienced a small taste of adventure in the opportunities that I created or came my way. In those beautiful moments of breaking out of the constraints of everyday life, I experienced life-changing moments.

But many people occasionally settle for an exciting moment, then go back to their safety net of comfort. After all, that is the rhythm of life; why try and disrupt it? But I wanted those exciting, adventurous moments to be a part of my everyday life, not just a fleeting once in a blue moon experience. I want to lay hold of all God has in store for me, knowing that I am living my life to its full potential. Organising the Empower event helped me to understand that in order to have these experiences, I had to be willing to fight for them. I have always fought hard in every area of my life. Nothing has ever been handed to me. Career-wise I felt I had little to show for my years of effort. People that know me would say this is not the case. Maybe that is true, but sometimes it is hard for me to believe. All I want is to live a meaningful life doing what I love, hopefully making a living from it. And for the fruits of my hard work to bring success and blessing for my family and me. And to bless and help other people.

A few well-meaning people suggested on a few occasions that perhaps I should team up with a White person as the face of my business to get more opportunities. I was mortified by such an idea. Why should the colour of my skin be seen as something negative? These types of comments upset me, and at times knocked my confidence. It was on a particular day after such a comment that in a pre-scheduled evening phone call with Celina, I told her why I was upset. We never usually had these types of conversations. My guard was down that day. But nevertheless, she was very encouraging. She told me, like my mentor Cheryl had, that in another part of the world, my hard work would be valued and appreciated. I was prepared to wait for the day all my hard work would pay off.

My battle with internalising what I perceived to be external professional rejection reared its head from time to time. But I trusted that God had a plan for my life, better than I could imagine. Time and time again, God showed me that He had given me the ideas, tools, and intelligence to create my own table of opportunities. As experience has shown me, it is rare for others to let you pull up a chair to sit at their table. In those moments of insecurity, it served as an important reminder not to seek the validation of man but to seek approval from God.

CHAPTER SIX
RUBBER BAND FAITH

One morning after my prayer time, I felt led to contact a lady called Judith. This was not the first time I had an impression to do this. At first, I shrugged off the thought, as it seemed like a strange thing to do. I had only met Judith once at a speaking engagement I had done at a church two years before. My friend Andrena had invited me to speak on my journey to healing from childhood sexual abuse. Anyway, I sent Andrena a message via WhatsApp to ask Judith to contact me. I was sure Judith would be puzzled as to why I messaged her. I was not sure she would respond. But to my surprise, Judith contacted me the same day. She had just finished reading my book *Daughter Arise* (that she purchased two years before at the event I did at her church). And she was also in the process of contacting Andrena for my details. I was shocked at the timing of it. I knew then this connection was God-led.

God-incidence. That is what Judith and I called it. We could not believe the timing of our contact but knew it was for a reason. We exchanged email details and began to correspond shortly afterwards. The emails from Judith encouraged me. Her words of concern and empathy transcended through the tone of her words. She wanted me to know that she was praying for my family and me. I told her about my journey since writing my book *Daughter Arise* and my efforts in putting together the Empower event. I asked Judith if she could help me fundraise for the event. She said she would pray about it and let me know.

Despite the lack of donations, other aspects of the event were coming together nicely. I found my first speaker for the event via Twitter. Misty Griffin, an advocate for child victims of sexual abuse, had done a lot of work over the years in Los

Angeles to raise awareness. We followed each other on Twitter for years. I was always inspired by her bravery in sharing her own story of escaping sexual abuse in the Amish community. I decided she would be a great speaker for the event, so I sent her a private message. I was pleasantly surprised that she agreed. Again, it was exciting to see another positive result of doing something bold. Another lady, Jackie Linn, contacted me via Facebook all the way from Nevada, America. I was intrigued to find out how she heard about little old me from Southwest London, so I contacted her back straight away. I knew nobody in America apart from Celina in California. My ventures were not commonly known anywhere else either. I found out that Jackie had been doing a search for awareness events. She found me through a listing I posted on an online community event board. Jackie was a survivor of abuse, and she used her gift of singing to raise awareness and uplift other survivors. Alongside her partner Aquari Jones they performed as a duo. Jackie offered to provide the entertainment for the event as well as share her story. This was good news. Celina and I found it hard to source a singer and entertainment at a price within our budget.

We decided after listening to her music that Jackie would be a good addition to the event. It was a blessing to now have all the speakers, organisations, and entertainment in place.

To save money, I designed the program for the event using a template I found online that I could easily adapt using my MacBook and printer. It proved quite tricky to do. After seeing the quality of the printed program, I decided to get them printed via Instaprint. I ordered 120 programs in colour. The plan was to send the package ahead of my trip to Celina.

I was proud of my innovativeness and creativity. I worked diligently and put careful consideration into every detail because I wanted the guests to feel special. My daughter Jada was such a blessing to me during this time. I always involved her in tasks to do with my businesses. I want her to see the result of hard work. Jada always offers to help and would do anything I ask her to. She is intelligent and very creative. And always has suggestions on getting things done in a minimum amount of time. I have learned a lot from her. To reward her, I paid her for her work. Her input helped me cut out unnecessary tasks.

Judith got back to me a couple of weeks after our initial emails. She agreed to help me fundraise for the Empower event and came up with an idea called wear it, love it, and share it. For the price of an entrance ticket, the ladies could bring clothing items they did not want and swap them for something they liked. The fundraiser was held a couple of weeks later at the same church I visited to do the speaking engagement two years before. The event had a great turnout, and Judith and her team of helpers put so much effort into the evening. They made fruit cocktails and an array of different healthy snacks for the guests to nibble on. Also, there were stands of homemade craft items that people could buy. Judith is very creative. I was amazed to see what she made. Handbags, pencil cases, and lunch boxes were made from recycled crisp bags, milk cartons, and toothpaste tubes. The items were in popular demand and sold out by the end of the evening. The ladies were also pleased with their clothing purchases. In total, £380.00 was raised from the event. Again, I was reminded to trust God. Even when I thought it was silly to contact Judith, there was a reason behind it.

To further support me on my mission to complete the event, my friend Andrena set up a WhatsApp prayer group with a few of the ladies from the church. This was a real support to me. Anything I needed prayer for, I could message them, and they would pray for me. The group really gave me the strength to continue and encouraged me to keep going.

Phone meetings between Celina and I happened less and less. We would arrange to talk, but Celina would cancel or re-arrange because of work or personal commitments. I could understand because I was also battling with the same pressures. However, with the event now three weeks away, I had to make it my priority. To ease the pressure, I emailed Celina to ask her if she needed any help with the tasks she was meant to do. I figured if I could help with the outstanding tasks, it would give her some breathing space. Her replies to my emails were also sporadic. I started to panic. I admit. And that came across in my frequent emails to ask what was going on. I did not help the situation, and Celina did not appreciate it. She felt I was panicking for no reason and said I was taking the fun out of her being involved in the event. She kept saying to trust her, but how could I trust with no communication?

For me, the event was not fun at this stage; it was work. I had a lot on the line, including my reputation. I had a responsibility to put on a professional event. It did not matter if I was a volunteer or not. People had expectations that I would deliver what I promised, and I could not go back on what I said I would do. With three weeks left, there was still so much to do and money to be raised. How could this communication breakdown be happening at such a critical time?

With hindsight, I could see there were a few problems. Firstly, relying on email to communicate a range of different things, including thoughts and feelings, was a huge mistake. It was easy for the tone of wording to be misconstrued as something else. Secondly, I think we both viewed our relationship differently. The boundaries of our relationship were not clearly defined. We went from a client/service user relationship to co-partnering on an international event. For me, it was a professional relationship, but for Celina, she was helping a friend. Celina has a good heart and really wanted to help make the event a reality, but even with her best intentions, it possibly may have been too much to handle. No matter how I tried to rectify the situation, I only seemed to make it worse. I take full responsibility for how things turned out. I decided not to contact her for a while with the hope that the situation would change.

So, with Celina not in the picture, I was responsible for planning, coordinating, and managing the event on both sides of the Atlantic. The weight was heavily on my shoulders. Because of the time difference, this meant I spent many late nights calling people in California to finalise the arrangements. Sometimes I would go to bed at 11:00 pm and set my alarm to get up at 3:00 am to have phone meetings with Jackie, the singer I hired for the event. She lived in Arizona, and the time difference was different from California. It was calling her to check what equipment she needed to perform when it became apparent that the PA system at the venue was inadequate. At the very least, I would need to hire a DJ because he would have all the right equipment. Another expense was the last thing I needed. I was already finding it difficult to raise the initial money and now having this unforeseen expense was a problem.

Nevertheless, I told Jackie to find a DJ, as I knew no one in California, let alone Rancho Cucamonga. This event needed serious prayer. It seemed to be going pear-shaped. I decided to bring the situation to the attention of the ladies' prayer group.

I started to feel down about the event. Doubts about whether I was meant to take on a task of this magnitude returned. Why couldn't things be straightforward? Overwhelming fear visited me each morning as I woke up. I found it hard to get out of bed some mornings. How was I supposed to oversee an international event without help? I had no one that was my eyes and ears on the ground anymore in California. Even with my great organisation and planning skills, there was no way I could pull it off. Not only was there the issue of logistical planning, but I also now had to find somewhere for my daughter and me to stay. Easy you may think. But the problem was I now had to find out where the venue was and book somewhere near that was easy to get to. I had to also find a Costco to buy all the food and arrange transportation for it. I would also need a place to store all the food, equipment, and material. And, I now had to pack and bring the leaflets and other event items with me as part of my luggage. I could not help but feel hopeless the more I focused on the issues. With each passing day, I found it hard to believe this event would become a reality.

Rubber band faith. That is what is required. God used a sermon by Jentezen Franklin to show me that the situation I was facing was right where I needed to be. This was a test of faith. Like a rubber band, I was being stretched beyond my limits. It was the stretching that required me to dig deep and push through. It was the stretching that caused me to pray, as I had never done before. Being stretched caused me to rise up and think outside the box. Rubber band faith meant I had to rely on God to provide a supernatural miracle because everything was out of my hands. This was God's territory. And this was evident in the mighty exploits and stories of Elisha, Moses, Jesus, and even Jackie Pullinger. God gave them success in all they did because of their courageous faith and His supernatural providence.

I had experienced the results of great faith before, but this was different. I was being taken to the next level. To trust in a way I had never known. It really did require me to step out of the boat. It was excruciating. Most mornings, I called my friend Pauline to talk, cry and pray. She was such a support to me during this time. Besides Cheryl, Pauline was the only other person that encouraged me to continue to push forward with the event and not give up. Their support and the sermon on having rubber band faith strengthened and encouraged me to have faith and hold my resolve. Other well-meaning people saw the challenges and took it as a sign that God was telling me to give up.

But there was no way I would cancel the event. People depended on me. Organisations believed in what I was doing and volunteered staff to support the event. Tickets were slowly starting to sell. I could not let people down. Of course, people would probably say they understand, but that's not the point. I am a person of my word. If I say I will do it, I will. God showed me years ago through Daughter Arise, my charity support group that I run for survivors, that even if only one person comes, I should go. The principle is the same. Only a few tickets had sold, but I was to go ahead with the event. Now was not the time to turn back. Instead, I decided to close my eyes and take the biggest leap of faith I had ever made. Fear was now the energy I used to push forward.

Fourteen days to go, and I had no place to stay during my trip to California. In the beginning, Celina had offered me a place to stay. But I guessed from the no response to my emails I would have to make alternative arrangements.

Cheryl told me about using air BnB as alternative accommodation to a traditional hotel. I had vaguely heard of air BnB's before, but I was not familiar with how it worked. I went on the website and searched for a place to stay in the area I wanted. The very first house I found was lovely. I contacted the owner to ask a few questions about the proximity to the venue and Costco. It was a good thing that I checked the information beforehand. I came to find out that to get to all the places that I needed was a drive away. This was very different from how it looked when I did a search on Google map. I decided to go ahead and book the accommodation. I figured I could always take an Uber to get me to these places. Victor and Adrianna, the hosts, confirmed that the available dates were being booked quickly. But I had a minor problem. I was awaiting payment from one of my contracts that was due in a few days. I told them I would get back to them later that day. I wondered how I could work it out. I needn't have worried. That afternoon I received a phone call from my friend Pauline. She offered to pay for my accommodation as a gift. She told me God had placed it on her heart to do it a few days before. I continued to be amazed and surprised by the people God put in my life to support me in what He called me to do.

I could not believe I had made it this far. I was so sure that Celina suddenly withdrawing from the event would be the final nail in the coffin. As I thought about how the situation with Celina had unfolded, I gained a different perspective. What if she was only meant to accompany me on this journey into the unknown thus far? What if she was just meant to be the catalyst to get me moving, to hold my hand to a certain point? God knew that I would never have attempted to go to another country without knowing anyone. Of course, to look at the situation at face value, especially with all the challenges, I would not do it. The more incredible the incidents of God's provision and seeing His hand move supernaturally in putting everything together, I was swayed to believe this was likely to be the case. I will always have appreciation in my heart for Celina. Her encouragement and passion for the vision I shared with her really encouraged me. God used her to open my eyes to see that His plan for me went beyond the borders of Brixton and London. God was indeed enlarging my territory and taking me to other parts of the world.

Eight days to go, and the fundraising target was still not met. I didn't know what to do. I had written to churches here and abroad for help, but I had no response. It was at this point I contacted Angela (manager of the hall I ran the support group from) to ask if the board members would consider donating. They responded that they couldn't donate, as they had community projects they supported. However, they suggested I come along to one of their church services to present my project to their members to see if they would donate.

A few days later, on a Sunday, I went to St. Paul church in Brixton to tell the congregation about the Empower event. I weary at this point. I didn't hold much hope of anyone donating. My attitude could be perceived as negative, but with what I had experienced so far in terms of giving, it was an indicator that sexual abuse was not a cause people readily gave money to. After the songs and notices, I was introduced to the congregation. I told them of the work I had done in the community over the last several years and my connection to St. Paul's because of the support group I ran at the hall. As I was speaking about the impact of sexual abuse, I was overwhelmed with tears. It dawned on me as I stood there that survivors of abuse really had to fight for everything. The fight to be believed, the fight to prove the damage it has on their life. The fight to get people to believe it is an injustice. The trauma of the child that later becomes the scars of the adult society seem to care little for. I felt the vulnerability of the cause and the loneliness of my past journey. I asked with boldness and passion for them to consider giving.

And gave they did. As I stood by the door at the end of the service, people came and put donations in my tin. They also encouraged me, uplifted me with kind words, and prayed for me. I was moved by their generosity in action and spirit, and it had been the first reminder I had in a long time of what church support meant. On leaving, I promised to return and update the congregation on the event. In total, they gave 307.00 pounds. I was so grateful.

My daughter and I spent the last few days packing our bags and preparing for our trip. We made all the name tags for the food, packed the programs, my books to do a book signing, and our clothes. I had done everything I could physically do. I worked hard and tried my best to salvage the event. It was all in the hands of God now, as it always was. All the donations I collected I changed into US dollars. I never reached my donation target, but I was confident God would help me stretch the money and provide the rest. It was now time to turn my focus to the unknown place I was going to. The adventure was about to begin.

CHAPTER SEVEN
DREAM BIG, FLY HIGH

The night before my trip, I could not sleep. A million thoughts raced through my mind. I was nervous and excited at the same time. I wondered what California was like and how the event would come together, and if ticket sales would pick up at the last minute. I promoted the event the best I could by posting on event listings online everywhere in L.A. The only outstanding issue was I had no volunteers to serve the food. I contacted churches in the community where the event was being held, but I got no response. After a long search online, I contacted an organisation called

Volunteer Corp. They provide volunteers for public events. As I contacted them at short notice, they could not confirm whether it was possible to send anyone. As a last resort, I emailed the organisations participating in the event to ask if they could help. All I could do was wait and see.

I also thought about whether the accommodation I booked was as nice as in the pictures in the listing. I was not worried: I was sure it would be okay. Because even in choosing a place to stay, I believed God had his hand in the process. I realised this when booking the accommodation. After I had made the booking, the first church I googled to find volunteers in their area, a picture of Vincent and Adele popped up! All these awesome moments that most people would believe as coincidences were a supernatural hug from God that He had ordered my steps.

My mind also thought about what American food tasted like. I had heard so much about In and Out, a California burger bar that everyone reckoned was so good. Personally, I was looking forward to trying Chick-fil-a, a restaurant that did all things chicken. Amid my flurry of random thoughts, I had a sense of peace about everything. In the quietness of my morning prayer, I knew God would not leave me or forsake me. After all, I had risked it all to follow Him in blind faith. Yet, I knew I had to trust Him a little more as I stepped deeper into the unknown.

My husband was just as excited as Jada and me on the morning of our trip. He helped us with our bags to the tube station, and we said our goodbyes there. In a way, it was sad that he didn't want to come on this adventure with us, but I could see he was looking forward to having his own time. That was natural, considering we had not spent more than a few days apart in fourteen years of marriage. A week would pass very quickly.

A sense of relief washed over me once we checked in for our flight. No hiccups in travel, and I had not forgotten anything. It felt like a huge burden had been lifted off my shoulders in leaving London behind for a while. Since leaving traditional paid employment in April 2018, everything had been non-stop in terms of activity. As much as I was enjoying my new entrepreneur journey, at times, it was like living in a pressure cooker. It was a rollercoaster of ups and downs, financial challenges, trying to figure out the best path to take in building my business, working contracts, alongside organising an international event. I really needed a break from everyday life. Not that this was a holiday, but at least I could focus on this one task without other responsibilities. No doubt other challenges would be waiting for me once I got to L.A. But for now, just for a few hours, I could forget about it.

Jada spent most of the flight watching movies. She was so excited to have the window seat. Every so often, Jada would marvel at the clouds. It had been a while since we last got on a plane, hence why she found it most exciting. It was nice to spend this time with her. In between reading the new book, I brought especially for the flight (*Les Brown, Live your dreams*). We spent our time laughing and talking about some of the funny things we had seen so far.

Once we got through customs at LAX airport, we decided to find a place to eat. My daughter requested In and Out burger, but we came to find out that the nearest branch was a 15-minute cab ride away in the opposite direction to where we were going. The airport did not have many food outlets. In fact, we could only find a small Starbucks shop tucked away down two flights of escalators in the corner. The selection was dire, to say the least. The sandwiches looked like the day had gotten the best of them. Rather than expose us to a dodgy stomach, I brought us two bags of crisps and a tub of grapes. Even the grapes looked unappealing and tasted a little sour, but we were hungry, so we ate them. I promised my daughter that once we got to our accommodation, I would find a burger shop. By this time, it was now 7:00 pm in the evening.

Remember I said about challenges awaiting me on my arrival in L.A? Well, I was about to experience my first one. I was trying to order an Uber, and my payment card kept declining. I had money in both my bank accounts and on my Post Office cash card. I was shocked this was happening, and of course, being hungry and tired from an 11-hour flight did not help my reaction to the situation. I had a bit of a meltdown but soon gathered myself together. I called the owner of the air BnB where we were staying and asked for advice. Whilst I was trying to figure out what to do, my level-headed daughter asked a driver parked in the waiting area what company he drove for. Because she wanted to find an alternative to

Uber, he suggested to her that I download an app called Lyft, an equivalent to Uber. She relayed the information to me at the same time Vincent had also made the same suggestion.

After downloading the Lyft application to my phone, I was still having problems booking a car with my bank card. For the life of me, I couldn't figure out what the issue was. As I tried my Post Office card again, I said a little prayer under my breath, hoping it would go through this time. This time I remained calm as I could see my daughter watching. To my surprise, my card went through with no problems. Our driver Chloe was a few minutes away from picking us up. I was so relieved. I had no idea what the next option would be if my card had failed.

It was now coming up to 9:00 pm at night. As we put our luggage in the boot, we were happy to finally be on the last part of our journey. Jada fell asleep within minutes of getting in the car. Just as well really. Our destination Upland, California, was an hour away. The map I viewed didn't really convey the distance between all the States and how big California was. I was surprised at how far our accommodation was from the airport. As Chloe was driving, it dawned on me that you do need a car to get around L.A.

For most of the car journey, Chloe and I made small talk. She asked me about the reason for my trip to California and how long was the duration of my stay. I told her about the Empower event and how I came to do work supporting survivors. Chloe told me she was a survivor of childhood sexual abuse and that most of her friends were survivors. It was another jaw-dropping God moment. What are the odds? I fly thousands of miles to a country I have never been to before, download a random taxi app on the advice of a stranger, order a car from the company, and the first driver that takes our ride is a survivor of childhood sexual abuse. It was a surreal moment. Because whilst I was getting a ride, I realised I was already doing the work I was called to do.

I admired her strength as I listened to her story. Mind you, because I had now seen a day and a night in the space of twenty-four hours, and my focus skills were seriously being put to the test. I was exhausted. At times, during the quiet pauses of reflection during our conversation, I closed my eyes only to be awoken by my own snores! I did not want Chloe to think she was boring me, and it was important that I listened, so I tried different things to keep me awake. I opened the window, but my daughter told me to close it, as she was cold. I shuffled my bum from side to side on the car seat to stop me from getting too comfortable. I pulled my chair up straight. As it was slightly leaned back, it only seemed to tempt me to sleep. I also aimed my concentration on the different road signs as she drove down the highway.

Chloe was surprised to hear that I had been married for fourteen years. She commented it was rare to hear about a survivor that has sustained a long-term relationship. All her friends' relationships had either ended in divorce or broken down due to issues stemming from past abuse. I was sad to hear this but knew from experience that relationships are hard to build with unresolved past trauma. Healing of self is always the first place to start from but not the easiest step to take. It requires a lot of courage to be openly vulnerable about things that have caused great pain.

I took the opportunity to tell Chloe about what Jesus had done in my life and how God turned my life around. I also told her where she could buy my

books and invited her and her friends to the event.
Chloe was not sure she could make it because she
was working but promised to pass on the flyers
to her friends. My encounter with Chloe was not
what I expected in my first interaction with a
person from L.A. to be like. Nevertheless, it was an
unforgettable experience and further brought home
to me the importance of what I was doing. Chloe
confirmed this type of event was not a common
occurrence for survivors in L.A.

Vincent was waiting to greet us by the front
door. He helped us inside with our bags. As we
entered the front room, we were greeted by a big
greyhound dog called Russo, who seemed excited to
meet us. Vincent introduced us to his wife, Adele.
They also had a son, Matthew, but he was fast
asleep. My daughter and I were so touched to find
that Vincent went out and brought us In and Out
burgers and fries. It was not expected but very much
appreciated as we were both hungry. Their home
was beautiful, spacious, and tastefully decorated.
We hit it off straight away with Vincent and Adele.
We spent the next couple of hours talking about
America, Trump, the Royal Family, amongst other
things. By the time we went to bed, it was 1:00

am. Our room was lovely, clean, and comfortable, with lots of space to store our belongings. My daughter and I shared a double bed, but as we are both at times terrible sleepers, we decided to sleep top and tail. After a much-needed shower, we both fell asleep straight away. We had finally made it to California.

There was no time for sleeping in as we wanted to make the most of our time in Upland. After unpacking our luggage and taking a shower, we decided to go out for breakfast. Vincent told us of a few places we could eat and drew us a map on how to get to them. I was useless with maps, but his drawing of the directions made sense. He offered to take us shopping for the event in the afternoon after he finished work. These kind gestures were typical of Vincent and his wife, Adele. They made us feel welcomed from the start and were always there to answer our questions.

I cannot begin to explain how truly beautiful Upland is. As Jada and I made our way to find the breakfast spot suggested, we were amazed at the beautiful mountains that served as a backdrop to the lovely houses with large front lawns that lined the spacious and quiet streets. Palm trees were in abundance everywhere that lined and complimented the clean and wide roads. As the sun shone brightly in the sky, I felt the stress leave me. This was what I needed.

American food portions are huge. We ordered French toast with streaky bacon, scrambled eggs, and apple juice. When the food arrived, the French toast was sprinkled with icing sugar and what looked like a scoop of ice cream. I was puzzled as to why they would serve bacon, egg, and ice cream together. It was not a combination of food I had heard of before. After politely inquiring with a guest on a table next to us, we found out the scoop of ice cream was butter! Discreetly, I scraped it off my bread, and then I proceeded to eat. I only ate the bacon, egg, and one slice of toast. Jada managed more than me, but we both enjoyed it. After I paid the bill, we decided to take a long walk to work off all the food we ate.

Our walk back to our accommodation was just as interesting as the walk to get breakfast. We saw large oil tankers, places of local interest and even found a 7-Eleven shop. We used to have 7-Eleven stores in London in the early nineties, but they closed. The people we came across were polite. That was one thing I noticed about American people. They were always courteous and willing to help. The roads were a bit confusing to cross as there were so many lights in different directions. Even when the pedestrian lights signalled green, we ran quickly across the road! We took pictures as we strolled along as Jada wanted to share her American adventure with her friends. I took fun pictures of her posing with flaming hot Cheetos and tried to take a picture of her in the middle of the road to catch the mountain as a backdrop. I failed miserably at taking the perfect picture. I was scared a car would come around the corner at any minute. It was nice to enjoy a different pace of life, even if it was only for a short while. We had fun in the sun and enjoyed every minute of it. We both agreed that Upland, California, was a place we could see ourselves living. We were sure that Stephen would like it. One day I made a silent promise to myself that I would bring the three of us back for a holiday.

We spent the afternoon chilling in our room, waiting for our hosts, Vincent and Adele, to finish work so that we could go shopping for the event. Whilst Jada watched videos on YouTube, I spent time on my laptop working on the final touches for the event. I checked the ticket sales, and a few more had sold since I arrived in California; in total, ten tickets had sold so far. With one day to go until the event, I remained hopeful there would be a surge of sales or that people would turn up and pay at the door.

Vincent and Adele were such a blessing to me during this time. They took us everywhere we needed to go and even made better suggestions on where to get things. There was no way I could have gotten around without them. Even the shops that looked close together on the map were a car ride away. We went to Costco to buy the food for the event. The sandwich platters were more expensive than I had anticipated. Because I didn't reach my fundraising target, after much discussion with Jada and Adele, we decided that it would be cheaper to buy the stuff to make the sandwiches. I managed to get everything I needed, and Vincent and Adele let me use their Costco card. When we went to get items from other shops, some were sold out. Even when I wanted to give up and leave something behind, Vincent and Adele encouraged me to try another shop. We did not stop until every item was purchased. After all our efforts, we stopped to get some well-deserved food. Jada opted for a different In and Out burger (burgers are her favourite) whilst I got a Chick-Fil-A. It was delicious and better than anything KFC could come up with. By the time we got back to our accommodation, it was 10:00 pm. After I unpacked all the items and prepared the bags and boxes to take to the venue for the next day, I climbed into bed, exhausted just after midnight.

As I lay in bed, I reflected on a productive but busy day. I was grateful that God took care of all the finer details of my trip. There was no way I could have foreseen or planned to get a shopping trip of this magnitude together in a foreign country. I wouldn't have known where to start or where to go. I needed someone who lived in the area to help me out. That is why I believe God sent Vincent and Adele my way. Not only for practical help but also to encourage me. Their support was more than I could have asked for or imagined; it was invaluable.

It felt like I had only been in bed five minutes when my phone alarm vibrated on the bedside table to alert me it was 5:00 am. I hit the snooze button once but knew if I hit it again, I was in danger of going back to sleep. I jumped out of bed. As my feet hit the floor, I felt like I had done a full gym workout, as every muscle in my body was sore and tired from pulling and carrying heavy bags and boxes since the beginning of the trip. My eyes burned with tiredness. I struggled to gather my thoughts together-to prepare for a long and demanding day. As for my daughter Jada, she was oblivious to the noise I was making as I searched around for the things I needed to get ready. I thought about how precious it would be to sleep for a couple more hours.

But there was no chance of that. Time was already creeping by, and I had five hours to get everything ready. After I showered, I made my way to the kitchen to start making the sandwiches. This was not something I factored into preparing for the event making sandwiches at 6:00 am in the morning, but desperate times called for desperate measures. This was nothing new to me. I had made large quantities of sandwiches twice before for other large-scale events I had organised in the past. Rather than sulk about it, I rose to the challenge and did what I needed to do.

I sought the advice of Vincent and Adele on what type of sandwiches I should make. I guessed cucumber sandwiches would probably not be their thing. So, with eighteen loaves of bread, turkey ham, salads, cheese, and loads of cling film, I made a varied combination of sandwiches. At least I didn't have to butter all the loaves of bread this time, as Hawaiian bread didn't need it. On first hearing that Americans don't use butter on their bread, Jada and I were puzzled. How could they eat dry bread? But when we tasted it, it was the loveliest bread we had ever tasted! Soft, moist, and buttery. Much better than the bread we were used to in the U.K.

As I got into the rhythm of sandwich-making, I cut the crusts off with precision into triangles and neatly arranged them onto numerous silver foil platters. By the time I finished making the sandwiches, it was 9:00 am. Each person coming to the event would get a sandwich, a bottle of water, or a can of coke (apparently, this was the drink of choice apart from water that people liked). And a cookie or muffin and potato chips (crisps!). Considering it was only a four-hour event, they would be well fed. I was proud of myself for rising to the challenge with such calm and focus. I realised how much I had grown since preciously doing the same task five years before. Back then,

I admit I did not approach the task positively the second time doing it. But now I can see the day of small beginnings prepared me for a reason.

After I had made my daughter breakfast, we both finished getting ready. We took everything for the event out to the porch to be loaded into the car. There was so much stuff to bring to the venue. Vincent kindly offered to drive us there. Jada and I sat with trays of food on our laps as every space in the car was packed with stuff. The venue was only 20 minutes away, but it involved travelling on a highway. Again, I was amazed at the distance between places.

The venue was as beautiful as when I first saw it on the website. As the car pulled up, it felt surreal to be standing outside it. This was indeed the stuff dreams were made of. Hard work, perseverance, and the favour of God had now made it a reality. It was a hot and sunny day, perfect weather to come out to an event. The weather was my encouragement that things would turn out okay. I knew I would not have a full house but expected some people would come. I needed fifteen people to buy a ticket to pay the D.J. Otherwise, I would have to pay out of my pocket.

Some of the participants (apart from Misty and the San Bernardino Sexual Assault Services volunteers) were late because of traffic. I wasn't annoyed. It was a Saturday, and I expected the roads would be busy because of the weekend. The Volunteer Corp managed to send one volunteer; a man called Fernando. He was so helpful. Between me, him, and Jada, we set up the food and decorated the hall with efficiency. I was proud of myself. I was pleased with how I managed to organise and transition the event from England to California. Even under pressure, I had not forgotten anything. I had everything I needed.

Everyone involved in the event was now present, with ten minutes to go until it started. I gathered everyone around to thank them for volunteering to be a part of the Empower event. I was touched by the lovely words of support that I received. Everyone was so encouraging. The venue was ready, and the volunteers and speakers were prepared. The D.J completed the soundcheck. Now all that was needed was for people to come.

I knew something was not right when at 3:00 pm, the first guests arrived as the event was meant to start at 1:00 pm. With each hour that passed,

I felt discouraged. I kept apologising to those involved that gave their time so generously. I could feel tears welling up in my eyes. I was upset by what was happening. Still, I tried to maintain an upbeat composure, even though my demeanour showed otherwise, as I thanked the three guests that had travelled from another state to attend. I didn't understand why I had such a low turnout, that was until Misty and other participants informed me that it was Memorial weekend. Memorial Day is marked on the last Monday in May. It is a day that commemorates the men and women who died in military service for the United States. It is the equivalent to a bank holiday in England. They were shocked that I didn't know. How could I have known? They said Celina would have known as it is a national holiday. She never mentioned it to me. If I had known the importance of this date, maybe I would have suggested another date. Everyone knows that on a bank holiday weekend, most people usually go away for a short break. I couldn't believe it.

I felt like giving up at this point, but everyone encouraged me to keep on. I slipped away to the back of the hall and cried (out of sight of the guests). Some of the participants came and spoke words of reassurance to me. Jackie and Aquari (the singers) told me I was doing good work. They shared their story of how they started performing at venues. How the numbers of people that came to their shows were small, to begin with, but they kept going. They told me that whether the audience was three or three hundred, they would perform at the Empower event with the same passion and enthusiasm. Misty helped with anything I asked, and the D.J gave me a hug. But it was the words of my daughter, Jada, that uplifted me the most. She said, "I am proud of you, Mum. Look on this as a practice run. One day, your events will be selling out stadiums. I have learned a lot from you. You never gave up, even when everything was difficult. I love you."

Her words gave me the power to carry on. I realised that she was witnessing something through my journey and learning valuable lessons. Besides caring for others, she was learning about resilience, overcoming adversity, hard work. It made me realise that I had to refocus and finish strong.

As they say, the show must go on. All the speakers shared their information, and the personal stories from Jackie and Misty were touching. I shared my story of overcoming abuse and why it was important to support survivors that had not found their voice. As the event went on, I forgot about the number of people that came. Instead, I focused on making sure the guests had an event to remember.

No one turned up at the door, and I paid the D.J. out of my own pocket. But the feedback I received was amazing, considering all that happened. I was so exhausted but glad I did it. At the end of the event, there was so much food and drinks leftover that I asked everyone to take some home with them! Misty, Jada, and I were the only ones left at the end. We tidied up the venue, and Misty helped us take all the leftover food on a trolley outside as we had ordered a Lyft car to tack us back to the Air BnB. As we parted ways, I thanked Misty for all her help.

On our arrival back at our accommodation, we were greeted by Adele on the front lawn. Just by looking at me, she could tell it had not gone the way I had hoped. She gave me a big hug. It was Vincent's birthday, and both their families had come round to celebrate. They invited us to celebrate with them, but all I wanted to do was go to bed. I was exhausted and so disappointed. I just needed time to rest and reflect. Jada took their invitation and went and enjoyed the party.

I could not think of anything else that evening. I had mixed feelings about it all. All the people involved in the event were amazed and touched that I would fly across the world to put on an event for people I had never met. Some commented that my actions had impacted them. Yet still, as I lay crying in my bed, I could not appreciate or see the small but significant things that my actions brought in the lives of others. I only saw the adversity, the challenges, and the fight it took to get here. For all my hard work, it seemed such a small win.

The only words I could muster to say to God was, what was it all for? But I got no immediate answer. Maybe it was pride that I was expecting something more for my great leap of faith. Maybe, I was expecting a big breakthrough in my life for doing something as audacious and courageous as this. As Jada came in and out of the room to get various things, my mind replayed the journey it took to get here.

My husband, Stephen, WhatsApp messaged me a couple of times during the evening to ask how the event went. I vaguely mentioned it, promising to call the next day to tell him all about it. As he had spoken to Jada a couple of times during the evening, I think he got the picture. I felt embarrassed to tell him what had happened. Stupidly I assumed he would say I told you so. I don't know why I thought that. Maybe because it had been a battle for him to believe that this really was a call from God ever since I had stepped out on this journey into the unknown. From the looks of things on the outside, it seemed that common sense should have prevailed. But when all is said and done, despite my feelings, I knew God had a reason for sending me here, even though I could not see it.

The next morning (Sunday), I messaged my husband to tell him what happened. He sent me a beautiful message straight from the heart. A message that could only be sent from somebody that truly knows and loves me. He told me he was proud of me and that I should feel proud of myself. He also said I was brave and courageous for doing what I did because he knew no one else would have done that. Immediately upon reading his message, I felt better. We may not have seen eye to eye on how I got to the point of leaving my job, but when it mattered the most, he remembered that my heart was always in the right place.

For the rest of our trip, Vincent and Adele took Jada and me to some great places. Firstly, we attended their church with them. Abundant Life Family Church is a large church, but everyone made us feel welcomed. It was an experience I will never forget, as, during the service, Jada gave her life to Christ and became a born-again Christian. The visiting pastor invited people to stand up and make a declaration of faith. I was amazed that my daughter did this as she can be quite shy and reserved. The thought did cross my mind: what if this was the whole purpose of the trip? That Jada would be saved here? Could it be that this pastor was the only one that could get the message of the gospel across to her? God never gave me confirmation either way. Of course, if this was the reason, then it is worth it.

We visited Hollywood. Jada and I were shocked at the state of it in real life. Jada especially, as she thought it would look like it does on the T.V. Instead, it reminded me of Camden High Street. It was unkempt with lots of graffiti and had quite a few abandoned buildings. We were also shocked at the high number of homeless people that were living on the streets. We saw the famous Kodak Theatre and caught a glimpse of the Hollywood walk of fame where the celebrities have their stars. It was packed full of tourists, and you couldn't really walk around. We took a walk in the Hollywood Hills and saw other places. In the evening, we marked the end of our trip with dinner at a Chinese restaurant. We spent our last day shopping and relaxing in Rancho Cucamonga.

The next day Vincent dropped us at the Metro station to get back to LAX. Both Jada and I were sad to be leaving Upland. We had grown accustomed to the quiet way of life, the people, and the environment in such a short space of time. It was hard saying goodbye to Victor and his family. One day I would return. God knows when that will be. But it will happen.

CHAPTER EIGHT

GREAT THINGS I DID NOT KNOW

Through the different challenges, trials, and the different experiences I have had during my life so far, indeed, I have learned things about myself that I did not know. I never realised what I was capable of until I stepped into the unknown. For instance, I didn't realise how strong I was under pressure or that it would cause me to push through when the odds were against me. In every situation that I have stepped out into the unknown for, I have faced some type of character or life challenge (financial hardship, rejection, and isolation, to name a few). These situations could have caused me to break down or made me turn back to the comfortable place of routine and predictability from where I had come. Of course, it would have been far easier to accept the traditional pathway of the life that I was expected to live (9-5 job, career progression, following a certain path). But I never turned back. I held my resolve even though there were many times I felt circumstances would break me; I am still here!

Are you at a crossroads in your life? Do you want more? Do you believe you are capable of much more than your currently doing? Do you recognise the inner restlessness I shared with you throughout this book? That is because you have a desire to do more with your life. There is a reason why you ask yourself questions and feel this way. But the question is, is it enough to encourage you to explore what lies beyond your current life? Make no mistake, the journey into the unknown will cost you. But understand this, anything worth having in life comes at a cost. With that in mind, I want to share some great things I did not know that I learnt from my journey and experiences.

Comfort costs

That's right. You are not mistaken in what you've just read, comfort costs. I didn't realise this until AFTER I left my last traditional paid job. It all seems so cosy, doesn't it? The routine, predictability, and comfort of 'knowing' exactly what each day will bring. Beware, it's a trap. The very thing enticing you to stay can be the same thing that kills personal growth and delays you from achieving your dreams. The Groundhog Day of comfort can make the days pass by quicker or longer, depending on where you find yourself. Before long, you could miss the signs that it's time to move on.

Another danger that comes with comfort is that it can subtlety define your identity and impact how you view your capabilities and potential. I had a limited view of myself whilst working in traditional career jobs. I thought my self-worth and value came through them. If I could only be a "success" in my job, I would be promoted, accepted, and respected, thus validating that I was someone of "value". Over time, I subconsciously became conformed and conditioned by trying to tick organisational boxes and the pattern of following a traditional career to have comfortable modern living. This resulted in me feeling unhappy and disillusioned. You see, I discovered there is a cost for everything in life, good or bad. It's up to you which bill you are willing to pay. Whether it's taking a risk to try something new, staying in a job you don't even like to climb the career ladder, or just get a regular paycheque, it will cost you!

God did not put you on earth to service bills or to jump through people's hoops! Jesus came that you might have life more abundantly in Him. Anything less diminishes you. *"The thief does not come except to steal, kill, and to destroy. I have come that they may have life and that they may have it more abundantly"* (**John 10:10**). And God wants you to do great exploits on his behalf. *"but the people who do know their God shall be strong and do exploits"* (**Daniel 11:32**). I have witnessed too many times, people that have become bitter and negative because their life has been ruined by living in the comfort zone. Years, even decades later, they wonder where the time has gone and complain about their lot. Don't let that be you.

The first step is the hardest

When you decide to do something new, the first step is always the hardest. All sorts of thoughts will cross your mind. And often those thoughts will be on the side of caution, giving you reasons WHY you should not do it! As I have shared with you throughout this book, I have experienced many firsts. None of them was easy. But the most important thing I learned was that the first step was necessary because it is the catalyst for change and puts in motion the actions for the other steps.

It is totally normal to feel scared. It is normal to be doubtful over your decision to try something new. If you didn't have these feelings, I would think something was wrong! These feelings are a natural response to attempting to do something out of the 'norm.' The wonderful thing about the first step is that you can always re-adjust the other steps if you need to. It is also a great place to learn from. Don't stay in limbo about deciding to go for it; otherwise, you will talk yourself out of it. Take a deep breath and step forward.

<u>Courage is required</u>

To create a life change, you must have courage. Easier said than done, I know. That's why I was inspired to create The Courage Course, an online course to teach people about courage and help them develop an action plan. Courage is all about action, despite fear and doubts. I remember hearing Joyce Meyer, a famous Christian author, say, "feel the fear and do it anyway." Never has a saying been so true when it comes to having courage. Courage means moving forward when there is no clear sign of how things will work out. Having courage pushes you beyond your own capability and limits. It's certainly not an act of the faint-hearted, but the faint-hearted can make a bold move of courage.

I've done a lot of courageous things, starting from when I was a child. Some of my decisions paid off. Others have not. But they all came at some type of cost and required that I had courage. One of the big rewards I have reaped from courageous action is how I have grown mentally, emotionally, and spiritually as a person. Also, I have grown in confidence from stepping outside of my comfort zone. I have done things I never thought I could do or achieve. To get what you have not gotten before, to go to a new or different level in your life requires courage. There is no other way.

Seize the day

There is never going to be a perfect time to take a chance and step into the unknown. Circumstances will never be perfect. The timing may not necessarily be right either. Whilst it is good to be prepared, 'preparing' can become another distraction to take you away from seizing the opportunity. In my case, God called me to leave certain jobs at a particular time despite personal circumstances. I had a certain amount of time to seize my window of opportunity. Even though I was hesitant, had I waited or tried to figure out the whys, when and what's, I would have missed it. A good indicator that it is time to move is when you have a sense of urgency or a nagging feeling that does not leave you. Seize the day, don't wait. The outcome may surprise you in a way you did not expect.

The journey is lonely

One of the hardest things about the journey into the unknown is the feeling of loneliness. I felt isolated at times as I had no one around me that had attempted the things I had done. I remember reading John Maxwell's book, *The Journey to Success and Significance*. John mentioned that to achieve great things, the journey sometimes is a lonely road.

You may find your decision to break away from the confines of society living, family traditions, or doing something different from those around you will automatically cause tension. Early on in my journey, my decision to follow God was a bone of contention in my marriage. But I had a strong conviction that even though the journey would be difficult, I had to go through it. It takes a lot of strength to break away from the fold and not bow to pressure, but it can be done. God was my friend, strength, and comforter on my journey. He is all I need and walks with me daily. With faith in God, you can walk this journey and navigate the highs and lows of unknown territory too.

<u>You must be your biggest cheerleader</u>

When no one else is cheering you on or supporting you to walk in your purpose or fulfil your dream, you will have to find ways to encourage yourself. I found it hard, at first, not to have consistent support. But after a while, I allowed my aspirations to be my encouragement. And anyway, regardless of the circumstances, God is my encourager.

As long as you have a vision, self-belief, and passion, it will take you far. It is the fuel that propels your big idea, goal, dream, or aspiration. It will also get you through the tough times. Once you've empowered yourself, you will find the strength for each day. Even when I have been discouraged and disillusioned (there are many times I feel like this), my creativity and passion for helping people find solutions to their problems get me back on track. I also listen to podcasts, interviews and read books from other entrepreneurs. It encourages and helps me to understand that I am not the first person to walk this path; countless others have done it before me. All these things serve as my cheerleader.

People may not support you

In life-changing situations I faced in my life that have required me to take a risk, it has been a rare occurrence that people supported my decisions. It took me a while to not take it personally or be upset about it. I had to accept that it was okay if people did not support me. Why is it hard for people to support you when you do something different from what they expect? There are many reasons. When you look at it in the context that only a small percentage of people live life outside their comfort zone According to statistics by the British Heart Foundation, 2017, over half of Brits don't venture outside of their comfort zones, and almost half (45%) fear that one day they might live to regret it. It is not hard to understand. Many people find it difficult to support those doing something different from them. Personal fear and mindset, not having done something different themselves, often, play a part. It is understandable and does seem like common sense to stick with what you know. Without God, I don't know if I could have stood firm in my decisions for so long. But if you make the Living God and His son Jesus Christ your rock and foundation, you will stand firm. *"Therefore, whoever hears these sayings of mine, and does them, I will liken him to a wise man who built his house on the rock: and the rain descended, the floods came, and the winds blew and beat on that house; and it did not fall, for it was founded on the rock"* **(Matthew 7:24-25).**

Some people may be part of your journey, but it doesn't mean they will walk with you the whole way; others not at all. Seek and connect with God and where possible others that are trying to do similar things in their life. Will you stay true to your purpose, vision, or dream when people don't support you? Or will it cause you to give up?

<u>Finances will be affected…at times</u>

As mentioned, besides a lack of support, the lack of finances can test your staying power and resolve when you step into the unknown. One of the hardest parts of my journey into the unknown has been finances. This issue has seriously had me considering at times a plan B (going back to a temporary job), especially in 2020. The Coronavirus Pandemic has affected the world globally, and I do not know what the future holds for me as an entrepreneur. But I do realise if I am to stay committed to my vision of empowering people as an entrepreneur, my plan B, so to speak, will need to come from something I create using my ideas, skills, talent, and experiences as God has given me these gifts to create resources, services and wealth (Deuteronomy 8:18).

The pressure from these unexpected challenges has been unbearable at times. Admittedly, it was already challenging being a self-employed entrepreneur with a family, starting a business from scratch. I felt guilty at times for stepping out to set up my own business. I see first-hand how inconsistent income has had an impact on my family. I feel like this even though I know I am doing what God called me to do.

The money dynamics have caused me to ponder the 'should-a, could-a, and 'what if's.' Should I have saved money before leaving my last job? Could I have stayed a bit longer? What if I got it wrong? Then I remember leaving my job was a window of opportunity moment. I had already 'umm and ahh'd' for sixteen months about my decision and made one attempt to leave, but I backed out. It was of the utmost importance that I took action. I had to be courageous and trust God. Whilst I wholeheartedly agree that saving money is a wise financial discipline to have regardless of circumstances. There was no way I could have foreseen saving an amount of money to see me through a global pandemic that has lasted over a year!

Of course, I did count the cost. I knew in some way there would be financial difficulties but did not know to what extent. But I certainly could not have known the impact this pandemic has had on my newly formed business. Up until this global crisis, I was getting by day-by-day on a no-frills financial roller-coaster ride of covering needs and minimising wants. I understood and accepted this as part and parcel of starting a new business. But it became excruciatingly painful when the pandemic wiped out 60% of my income. It has been hard. There are days that I cried and struggled under pressure.

Because of the continuous struggles, I continue to question if I'm still going in the right direction (continuing as a self-employed entrepreneur) three years later. Just the other day after praying, I heard the words *"guide you with my eye"* **(Psalm 32:8).** I guess this is a sign that I am still on the right track and that I still need to trust God. But I must admit I feel weary.

The entrepreneur journey has had an impact on everyday life, but I take each day as it comes. I have been walking in faith, waiting for a breakthrough to the next level for a long time. It will take a miracle for me to not only survive but thrive during this difficult time. But I believe God is a God of the impossible. He is a way-maker. He will make streams in the desert and a way in the wilderness for me **(Isaiah 43:17-19).** Hopefully, I will have a testimony to tell you that I came through the other side. Right now, I am still in the eye of the storm.

The pandemic has further confirmed to me that nothing in life is promised. It has shown me that unexpected events can thwart our best-laid plans (savings, job security, life plans). Even with my hardships, I would still tell you to count the cost and move forward. *"For which of you, intending to build a tower, does not sit down first and count the cost, whether he has enough to finish it" (Luke 14:28).* You must understand that you will not have a total cost upfront, but give or take, there will be one. In this process, I would encourage you to take this in prayer to God. Ask, what will it mean to you, your family, and your life to step into the unknown?

If you can accept it may cost you financially to do something different or life-changing, you are thinking on the right track. Understand it is a risk. You will never know the exact cost of the sacrifice you will make. The key is to expect it.

Adversity has benefits

It may seem like a weird thing to profess, but adversity has benefits. I have found my life experiences have provided the training ground to build my resilience and overcome adversity; they have prepared me for stepping into the unknown. I want to share with you three things adversity has taught me. Firstly, to dig deep when circumstances are challenging. Secondly, to think outside the box to find solutions to problems. And lastly, adversity has helped me develop as a person and given me a different perspective on my circumstances. Hardship, pain, and betrayal are never nice experiences when you are going through them. But I have found in these tests and trials that my personal growth was established.

There will always be giants

Fear, discouragement, doubt, hardship. Procrastination and other giants will rise against you as you step into the unknown. These giants will either cause you to shrink back or move forward. The land of milk and honey (the life you desire to live) is yours for the taking, but you must pursue and battle for it. You must decide, are you going to listen to your doubts and the doubters? Am I going to give in to my insecurities and fears?

Reaching your promise land is not going to be easy. The giants are part of your journey and an important part of your story. For how can you have the smooth without the rough? How can you experience the highs without going through the lows?

The giants are part of the experience of stepping into the unknown. In the moments you consider turning back because of your giants, this is the time you should reflect upon how far you have come. Remember the times you thought, 'I'm not going to make it,' but you did. Or the time you doubted you could take the first step, but you did. Reflect upon your previous journal entries if you have one (if you do not have a journal, start one!). Document your wins (the things you never thought you'd overcome) to encourage you. There is nothing you cannot overcome. Giants are to be cast down, not feared. You just need a plan to defeat them when they contend with you in battle. You will win. It may take several fights, but you will conquer them one at a time.

Just because it is difficult does not mean it is not right

Some people that witnessed my difficulties on my journey into the unknown took it as a sign that I made a wrong decision. And I can admit, I had times where I thought the same! But now I understand, three years into my journey, through a deeper revelation of God and His word, that I am going the right way.

I used to have a mindset that always thought because things are difficult means I got it wrong. Or I did something wrong—for example, my entrepreneurial journey. I have been a self-employed entrepreneur for three years now, and it is still challenging. Every so often, I am bothered by the thought, are these difficulties a sign I am going in the wrong direction?

The answer is no. In this microwave world we are living in (meaning unless you produce results instantly, it is a sign of failure), many people think success should come quickly. And if it does not, you should ditch whatever you are doing and try something else. This mindset is wrong. As frustrating as it is at times, I know I have to be patient. My journey is challenging, but I see results, just not in the way I had expected. I guess that cultivating patience is part of my learning. I do not expect anyone to understand my journey, the process, or why I do the things I do. I must seem a sucker for hardship. But establishing my business and walking in the fullness of my purpose will be difficult for as long as it takes unless God shows me otherwise. Nevertheless, I continue to trust him, for he will not guide me where he will not provide.

If things are difficult for you, do not automatically think you are not on the right path. Let God be your guide, not your feelings or people. Most of the time, people will judge your circumstances based on their journey, but you are not on the same life journey as them. Do not rely on common sense, trust God in faith. He will not lead you astray. Common sense (the perceived right way) does not require faith (the assumed wrong way) because it involves believing for things you are yet to receive. Faith is trusting God for the things you cannot see **(Hebrews 11:1),** especially when things are difficult. Having the faith to trust God is not easy. It is developed over time through a relationship with Him and is tested by action. None one will ever be able to figure out why God does things the way He does, but we can trust His way is right because He is the sovereign God, creator of Heaven and Earth. Mans' way of doing things is not God's way **(Isaiah 55:8)**.

I feel empowered knowing that God wants me to dream big and fly high. Gods' confidence and validation is my permission to live a life of adventure, to live an empowered life. Because of this, I make choices based on things that will empower and advance me to live my life to its fullest potential and to use my gifts, talents, ideas, and experiences to empower and help others. No longer am I willing to accept the morsels of living a life of comfort. I totally reject it. And when I experience problems, I look for solutions to move forward. By the grace of God, I took control of my own destiny by making choices that brought me in line with His purpose for my life. Additionally, I have made sacrifices that no one else around me was willing to make because I want to live my life to the fullest. I want to achieve beyond what I can think, ask or imagine **(Ephesians 3:20)**. I want to accomplish all the dreams, goals, and aspirations that I have in my heart. I have invested in the bank of self-development by gaining knowledge, working on personal issues and habits, and exposing myself to new possibilities and opportunities. No paycheque, uncertainty about job security, my age, people's opinions, thoughts, or feelings will stand in my way. With hard work, prayer, and the approval of the Living God, walking in faith with belief in myself, I will continue to move forward. I hope in reading my book, you will realise you can do the same.

Now I know why I struggled to fit it in and had so many challenges throughout my life; it was for a reason. Usually, the people that God uses to do exceptional things are set apart. They are often misunderstood and go through seasons of obscurity. This has happened to me. It was okay to be misunderstood; I am at peace with it now. I know I am not everyone's cup of tea. Gaining an understanding of myself as a person and accepting myself has also helped me get comfortable with living life on my terms. I don't live my life for the benefit of other people, only God. I never used to be like this. Many years ago, because of the aftermath of my abuse, I was fearful of rejection. I had low self-esteem and low confidence. I never accepted myself. I allowed people's opinions to influence me. Now, things have changed. Through Jesus Christ, I have gained an understanding of who I am and discovered my purpose in life.

The journey into the unknown has been crazy. Speaking out as a child about my abuse, leaving jobs, getting on a plane to fly across the world to empower people I didn't know required me to have courage, faith, and a heart for risk. I was scared at times, and in all these situations, I never knew the outcome. But I wouldn't change a thing.

As I conclude my story, I want to encourage you. Never give up on your goals or dreams, no matter how hard it seems. Dream big, fly high. What is impossible for you is possible for the Living God. Jesus says that those who are in Him we will do greater things than Him if we believe in Him (**John 14:12**). If you don't know Jesus, I have left a prayer for you at the back of this book.

I do not regret stepping into the unknown. It has been a beautiful, challenging, and amazing journey so far. When you think about it, life, in essence, is a journey into the unknown. No one knows what tomorrow will bring. Enjoy and embrace the journey anyway. You will be richer for it.

Do you need a courageous action plan to achieve your goals and dreams? Check out The Courage Course on Thinkific.com https://theempoweredlife-ad5c.thinkific.com/courses/the-courage-course

Social media:

YouTube – Living The Empowered Life

Instagram – Yeme_empowerment

Twitter – Yeme Empowerment

Facebook – Yeme Empowerment

Visit www.yemeempowerment.com to see what services and resources we offer for solutions to your current challenges.

Also, you can check out the Living The Empowered Life Podcast on Apple iTunes, Stitcher, and Spotify.

Get in touch. I would love to connect with you!

<u>SALVATION PRAYER</u>

Dear Lord Jesus,

I am sorry for the things I have done wrong in my life. I ask your forgiveness. Thank you for dying on the cross for me to set me free from my sins. Please come into my life and fill me with your Holy Spirit and be with me forever. Empower me to live my life to the full through your Holy Spirit. Thank you, Lord Jesus, Amen.

Lightning Source UK Ltd.
Milton Keynes UK
UKHW020156031221
394997UK00009B/2748